LGBT and Catholic Doctrine

Introduction:

The human being is not easy to understand.

Made in the image of God Himself, he is the pinnacle of all creation and all other things that were created, exist for his sake. The human being is a mystery; we can never fully understand the human being, just as we can never understand God Himself, because the human being was made in His image.

Anyone who says that they know everything there is to know about God and does not need to learn anything new is in error. In just the same way, anyone who says that they know everything there is to know about the human being and does not need to learn anything new is also in error.

There are things we know about God; concrete things revealed by God in the world and which shall stand true forever. But we have not understood everything there is to understand, because God is always more than what we know of Him.

There are things we know about the human being made in His image; concrete things revealed through nature and affirmed by God’s revelation, which shall never cease being true, no matter how much the times should change. But we have not yet understood everything there is to know about the human being, because he was made in God’s image.

The human being cannot understand himself without knowing God, because the human being is made in God's image. If the human turns away from God, then he cannot understand himself, because he is himself a reflection of the One he turns away from.

In modern times, there is such confusion about the nature of the human being. The human being was made good, but he takes his good nature and abuses it for evil, because he is confused about his own nature.

He does what he ought to know is wrong, but he is convinced it is not wrong, because he is confused about his own nature. Entire societies voice approval and give their consent to the abuses of human nature, and their media is filled with presentations of such abuses in a favourable light.

Young minds are corrupted as people teach their sins to the next generation and God patiently waits for people to change, preferring to suffer than to bring down His just wrath, which must necessarily come for those who do not accept His mercy.

I am not talking specifically about homosexual acts; they are just one small part of the wider sexual revolution that has plagued the culture.

Jesus loves those who offend Him. He would rather

suffer a thousand hells than to lose even a single soul. He is the victim who suffers for all these things; His flesh being torn from Him as we torture Him with our sins. And yet He suffers this willingly; He would rather do this than to lose even a single soul from Him.

God is furious with the sins of this world and He does punish them; this is a certainty. But He does not love to punish; He does love to give mercy, however.

People do not understand God's heart. There are in fact so many people of religion who do not understand the heart of the One they claim to speak for, nor do they understand the Spirit that called them.

The devil is often the first person to insist on justice, and God is often the last.

Justice belongs to God, and people of religion are right to point it out. But justice was never more important than the saving of souls.

When Moses saw the crowds of Israelites going to worship the golden calf and pervert themselves with their idolatries, he took the stone tablets that had the Ten Commandments written on them and shattered them against the ground.

God offered to him to destroy them all for their sins and make a new nation from Moses alone, and Moses begged God for mercy for them. The people deserved to die for their sins, but God listened to Moses and allowed for the people to receive mercy.

When he went up the mountain the second time, his face shone with light and he had to cover it with a veil. He talked to God as one talks to a friend, not as one talks to a master or overlord. He argued with God and protested to God, and God put up with it as a friend and answered him back as a friend.

In the days of the roman emperors, people would fall flat on their faces without looking up when the emperor was in front of them, without speaking anything unless they were called to speak. The Chinese Emperors required people to bow down and knock their heads on the ground (kow-tow) in their presence, and those who violated court etiquette could be executed. This is how people treat overlords, but not how they treat friends. Moses talked to God as a friend and argued with God about things he was upset about, and God did not strike him down, but instead talked to him back as a friend.

Paul said that the veil that Moses wore that hid the light of his face after he talked to God, represented the covering that blocked the view of the Israelites from recognizing God when He came down to Earth to walk among them. Moses threw down the tablets and broke them, he then proceeded to kill only a small portion of the people in punishment rather than the entire number of those who sinned, as justice would have dictated, because God's mercy allowed it. God listened to Moses as a friend and allowed Moses to intercede on behalf of the people, so that the justice due to them by the law could be averted.

Moses understood God; it was those who followed him who had a veil that blocked their sight. He called on God as his friend and argued with him; it was those who had the veil who could not understand God as anything different than overlord or master.

Jesus said to the disciples 'I call you friends and no longer slaves, because a slave does not know what his master is doing'. Moses was God's friend and not His slave because he knew and understood the Person behind the law. The Pharisees were His slaves, because they insisted on following the law without understanding the heart of the Person from whom the law came.

The devil is often the first person to insist on justice, to insist on the law being applied and the due punishment being given; and God is often last, preferring to suffer any price than to let those He loves to be destroyed.

I feel like there is such a deep misunderstanding of God that touches the issue in this book very deeply. God is furious at sin and He surely does punish sin; but He does not enjoy it.

If you always insist to be treated fairly, to be treated with justice, to be treated with respect, to be given your due and right portion– then you can' t be His disciple.

I need to explain something here that will take some time,

In the War of 1812 in North America, some British officers who were imbedded with a particular group of Amerindian allies in Michigan territory that were fighting for the British against the Americans witnessed a unique practice of execution of prisoners; the American soldiers were made to sit down in a circle with the Amerindian warriors and chiefs, and the Amerindians would be discussing with each other in words that the Americans could not understand. The Amerindians treated them in a friendly manner and put food in front of them, and they were made to feel comfortable.

The Americans, thinking this meant that their lives were safe then felt relief and ate the food. And from behind them, Amerindian warriors would then strike them in the back of the head with a tomahawk and kill them together in an instant. They died with bowls of soup to their mouths, feeling relieved and happy. The British officers watching the spectacle came to understand that they were doing this because they wanted them to die in peace; without even knowing that they were about to die.

It was in great contrast to other Amerindians who tortured their victims, even perhaps for days, before killing them.

Fyodor Dostoevsky, the Great Russian writer of the 19th century, was once arrested under charges of plotting against the Czar and he was scheduled to be executed by firing squad. He waited for months for the day to come, and when it did, he and others were lined up in front of the soldiers who readied their guns to shoot them.

Right at that moment, however, a rider came on horseback to tell them that the Czar had pardoned them and they were going to be let go free.

Dostoevsky has an element of this experience hidden in his writing. In his novel *The Idiot*, there is a character who says that thieves are more merciful than states, because when a thief kills someone, it only lasts a few minutes and then it is over, but when a state kills someone, it coldly passes a legal sentence, puts the prisoner into a cell where he has no contact with others and can do nothing else than just think about his fate, and then the victim must spend months or years, waiting every day in anxiety and terror that the day of his death is coming closer each moment that passes and there is nothing he can do to get out of it.

Dostoevesky was the right person to put this in his character's mouth, as he had gone through the experience himself.

Augustine of Hippo in his great work *City of God* derided

pagan religions for all kinds of illogical things within their beliefs. At one point, he mentioned that pagans believed that the soul that died went to paradise and then returned back again to the world to live again.

Augustine derided this belief as an illogical superstition, because he said that anyone who went up to God and was told that he had to leave, go back to the Earth and suffer later, could never truly be in paradise.

If the person was in paradise, but told they were going to go back to the Earth and suffer later, then they could not truly be in bliss anymore. Only if they were told that they would be there forever, could they be in bliss. As long as they are told that they will still have to suffer, there will always be something lacking from their happiness. A soul that lived in paradise and yet was told that he was not going to be there forever, but he would go back to the Earth and be tested and suffer again, would never be in complete peace even in paradise- so Augustine said in refutation to the pagans and their illogical beliefs.

I don't know if Augustine ever realized the full implications of what he was saying: Jesus Christ was that soul prior to His Incarnation.

Dostoevsky was only in that prison for a brief period, but he thought that the thief who cut the throat was more merciful than this. How much harder even still is it

to know, not just for months or years,   but for all
eternity, waiting and watching for that day to come,
when you know you must suffer, not simply a firing
squad, but the worst tortures imaginable.

His Mother was told at His presentation in the temple
that her own heart would be pierced and her Son would
suffer. How much easier it would have been if this had
been kept away from her, rather than make her live
every day of her Son's life, knowing that the day
would come.

And yet how much easier this was for her, than it was
for her Son, who shuddered at the thought of the
sufferings of His mother and who had known these
things for eons, perhaps never to truly experience
paradise because of it. To see God and be in His
presence at all times, whether on heaven or on Earth
and yet not have His tears wiped away.

And yet He willingly followed this plan. The prisoner in
the cell has no choice and would escape if he could; but
Jesus could run away at any time and His own love
made Him a prisoner to stay.

What compels a person to do this? He knew what was in
store for Him, and yet He came down to the Earth
anyways. He knew that they were going to kill Him in
Jerusalem and yet He went anyway. He knew that Judas
was going to betray Him, but He did not point him out

to the other disciples and call on them to stop him. He knew that they were coming to arrest Him, and he did not choose a different place to pray, but went to the same place on the Mount of Olives. He had wisdom surpassing all human beings, and had the power to refute Caiaphas and all the accusers against Him, but He did not even open His mouth for one word in His defence. Pilate asked Him 'where do you come from?' after the people had reported Jesus had claimed to be the Son of God, because Pilate had superstitions and was afraid that maybe this really was a god, but rather than Jesus telling Pilate that He was God and came from heaven, He kept hidden from him, and thus forced the governor to give Jesus the same unfair treatment given to any common person in the roman empire executed for unjust causes. He could have called on God to send down His angels at any time and rescue Him, but He refused.

Anne Catherine Emmerich, in her reported visions of the Passion written by her physician, claimed that when Jesus was offered the cross, He embraced it in the way a priest embraced a new altar.

Why does He do this?

Mother Teresa said that she believed that Jesus' agony in the garden of Olives was more painful than the passion itself. She herself was a person who suffered great internal darkness and suffering in her life that was invisible to others, and she understood something of this.

What did Jesus experience on the Mount of Olives?

I don't know if this this is correct, it is just my own speculations:

Imagine the most precious of all people to you. Your spouse, your child, your parents, perhaps a very close friend or someone else. Imagine the people you care about most deeply, more than anyone else and these people die. It is painful.

Now imagine, that not only do they die, but you see these people transformed into monsters, they no longer turn back to their old selves, but they live out their days in a hideous state of hatred for you and all human beings, and they suffer eternally because of this. You love them so deeply, and yet this monster has taken over and destroyed their old selves, and the loved one you once had is forever gone and you shall never see this person ever again no matter what. Not in heaven, not on Earth– forever they are gone, the monster has taken over and you shall never again have your loved one back.

Jesus loves every human being in existence even more than parents loves their own child.

No one is permitted to know that their salvation is

secure until they see God in heaven. Until that day comes, no one may ever have certainty of their own salvation. And so it was that the apostles following Jesus were told multiple times by Him that one of them was going to betray Him, but without being told who it was, they thus were denied the certainty of their salvation. And so it was that Joan of Arc and other visionaries could not know for certain that their visions were really from God or not. And so it was that all of us are never allowed to know with certainty that we are really going to be in heaven in the end or not.

But for Jesus Christ Himself, did He go through this too? Did He also experience the insecurity of knowing that salvation was not certain?

But He is salvation; so how could this be?

He was never denied certainty that what He was doing really was God's will and that He was in a state of grace. It is impossible that He didn't know this. It is impossible that He didn't know that all the scriptures concerning Him were going to be fulfilled and that He would complete all of these things.

What caused Him anxiety and pain was not the uncertainty about whether He was doing God's will but it was something else.

Human beings to God, in a certain way are like God to human beings. To be deprived of human beings for eternity to God's perspective, is like the vision of the sinner in hell who is denied the sight of God for eternity. If Jesus died on the cross, and no human being came back to Him, it would be like going to hell for Him; His torments would be similar, because the one thing He wanted was forever denied Him.

I feel like it perhaps was about this that He was not allowed to see with certainty, and thus He went through the same things regarding uncertainty that human beings do in their lives about their own salvation.

Jesus loves human beings more than parents love their children. To Him, we are everything. If He can't have us, it is like being condemned to hell; deprived of the sight of His beloved forever.

I think it was this that He suffered on the Mount of Olives. Anne Catherine Emmerich said that in her visions she saw Adam coming to a cave after he left the garden of Eden and pouring out tears at what had happened to him, and that it was at the same spot that Jesus poured out His agony prior to Judas' arrival.

The devil came to him and tormented him. He was forced to watch the life of each person in history, but He saw them not as strangers, but as one looks at his closest most beloved of family members. And the devil makes him watch as He sees one person after another making the wrong choices in life and going away from Him, becoming monsters and suffering forever for their sins.

You cannot live even a single day without this person, and yet you are forced to watch and know that you will go for eternity without him. Jesus suffered in that hour watching souls go away from Him more than what souls suffer in hell when they are deprived of the sight of God. In the moment of an hour He was able to witness the infinite amount of time that passes in hell for each one of these souls, suffering as He watched every part of it, looking upon the human being He loved and filled with indescribable despair in the knowledge that He can never have him back again.

The devil comes to him and presents Him with the lives of these people and the magnitude of their wickedness,
 'How will you feel if I take this one away? What about this one? Or that one?'

 'Suffer for them all. Die for each one. Suffer for every sin that they commit and they still will not love you back. Die a thousand times for them, and they will still not come back. They will still continue on in their sins. They will still not thank you for what you do for them.'

 'Go through the worst tortures for them. Take up the cross and die on it again. You still can' t have them back. They are gone forever.'

The Holy Spirit plants seeds into cultures; every piece of artwork that is published in whatever form has a meaning to it that is known in heaven. Whether it be pagan religions or 21st century media, it is the same.

Britney Spears in her first song 'Hit me baby' is about a girl after a breakup with her boyfriend.

The song can also be interpreted in a different fashion. It is a song about God losing His beloved, watching in agony as they break up with Him, and get immersed into a sexualized culture that will transform them into monsters and bring them to hell.

Spears' lyrics all reflect Jesus' agony over the sinners He loses to hell for their sins with their bodies, who are being depicted in the music video; these sexualized teens heading for damnation are the ones He is speaking these things to. 'My loneliness is killing me!', 'When I am not with you, I lose my mind!', 'there is nothing that I wouldn't do', 'Tell me how you want it to be', 'you've got me blinded' …

Jesus looks at the sinners that the devil makes Him watch and says with tears in His eyes and sweat like blood from His head, 'Tell me how you want it to be! Whatever it is, turn to me in prayer and I will help you. I want to know it! Whatever it is, turn to me, and I will help you with it. I will wipe away every tear in the end.

But I beg you, come back to me!'

He looks at each individual one that is lost to hell, knowing them each individually as one knows His most beloved of persons and says in utter agony,

'Please, I don't want to lose you. I beg you… I beg you with all my heart… there is nothing else I want!'

'What am I going to do without you? How will I continue without you? You can't leave me here alone like this!'

And the devil torments Him, by showing Him that no matter how much He suffers for these people, He can never have them back no matter what.

Standing over Him in triumph, He says, 'You suffer for them, and look they still fight wars, they still blaspheme, they still hate their neighbour, they still beat their wives, they still do this, they still do that… why did you even create them? You make them all and suffer this much for them, and in the end, you still don't have them. I will show you people who take your sacraments and murder their brethren in wars, who fleece the poor, I will show you your own ministers abusing children, filled with arrogance and hoarding wealth… look, son of man, look and see, for they shall never give you more thankfulness than this for all that you did for them!'

'Love them to death, die for them again if you like, and

they still will never turn back and love you!'

This is not the normal suffering. When people suffer,
they still can have hope that the suffering will end. This
has no hope; it is as though hope could be slain. You
cannot continue even a single day without the person,
and yet you must continue forever without ever having
this person again.

You cannot stop loving the person. It is impossible for
you to let the person go. It is impossible for you to go on
one day without the person. And yet you know you
must go on forever like this.

Mother Teresa is right; this was a pain worse than the
actual nailing to the cross.

This is a mystery I have had difficulty in understanding.
How can Jesus ever enjoy paradise when there are souls
in hell? Is He able to stop loving them? Can He let them
go? Can He feel bliss in heaven while knowing the one
He loves so much, even just one individual, is forever
deprived of Him and He can never have him back no
matter what?

Perhaps even Jesus Himself did not understand how this
was possible, but He trusted in the Father even still and
knew that somehow it would be good in the end. Jesus
is learning about God and human beings too with us.

This is the heart of God. This is the person that Moses talked with on Mount Sinai, who he knew as a friend and his face beamed with light after he managed to secure mercy rather than condemnation for all of the people; it was after Moses did this, not before, that the text says his face beamed with light.

This is the God that so many people of religion still do not understand.

If you understand this, then everything else falls into place. Why does He embrace the cross like an altar? Why does He not command the angels to save Him? Why does He not tell Pilate where He came from? Why does He not use His wisdom to win the trial in front of Caiaphas? Why does He not run from Judas or pick Him out for the disciples at the last supper to lynch? Why does He not avoid going to Jerusalem? Why does He come down to the Earth in the first place? Why does the prisoner choose to stay in the cell to await the firing squad, when escape was always within his power?

The answer is found in that hour beneath the olive trees. To suffer these things is painful, but it is such a small pain in comparison with the thought of being deprived of us forever.

He was the tablets that were shattered by Moses when he came down the mountain and saw their sin with his own eyes. He was the words written by God that were broken rather than breaking the people instead.

Margaret Mary Alacoque said that Jesus told her that if a soul was thankful to Him, He would be willing to come down to Earth and die again for this soul. Alphonsus de Liguori said that if in the whole of history there was only one person ever created and that was you, Jesus would still come down from heave and die on the cross for you alone.

There is nothing else He wants. To be deprived of us for Him is like the sinner in hell deprived of the sight of God.

Catholic doctrine cannot be understood in any other way than with the understanding of this Person standing behind it all. Without the mystery of the cross, Catholic doctrine can never be properly understood. Not just about LGBT issues, but about any issue.

I want to write a book about the human being; about the beloved one made on the sixth day that all other things were made to serve. I am a faithful disciple of the One who lives within the church and follow all of its teachings, but there are many things that I think I understand differently from most people. In the event anything in this work is found in opposition to Catholic doctrine, then I reject it.

This book is an attempt at teaching Catholic doctrine about this very complicated issue under the light of the One who loved the world like this and with a desire to seek the Truth above all other considerations.

I wish to explain these things so that people may understand the law as Moses did without the veil, and not as the Pharisees did with the veil. Not just to know the letter of the law, but to understand and love the Person behind it. Without knowing Him, no doctrine of the church can properly be understood. There are many others who can write far more than I can, who have talents that I don't have that could write much more and more deeply. I am going to write about what I think I know about His Truth, in order so that in some ways, at least, this veil can be removed.

In the end it is my wish that people can know that they do not need to fear or run from the Truth, because the Truth has so much love for them.

I invite the reader to say a prayer with me at the end of each chapter.

Lord, we pray that you help us to have a better understanding of the church's teaching on this issue as well as to apply it within our own lives, as well as to assist others to apply it within their lives. We pray that you help bring light into darkness with regard to this issue. We ask for these things, if it is your will, in Jesus' name, Amen

Part I: Doctrine

I: Scripture and Tradition

The Catholic Church has consistently always taught that homosexual acts are intrinsically immoral. It is in the catechism, it is in magisterial documents and it goes back to the apostles.

There is no record in the gospel of Jesus speaking directly on the subject but that doesn't mean He never spoke on it when He was walking the Earth, it only means that if He did, it is not mentioned in the gospel.

In the bible, there are several places it is mentioned directly.

The most important references are not direct, however, since they are the clear references in scripture that speak of marriage between a man and a woman. Whether it is the narrative of Adam and Eve in Genesis or John's recordings in Revelation about the Bridegroom marrying the Bride, the heterosexual nature of marriage is clear in scripture and in the gospel itself.

As far as direct references to homosexuality are concerned, there are the following:

The first is in the story of Sodom where the angels,

disguised as men, are told by the men of Sodom to come out of Lot's house so that they can have carnal relations with them. Lot attempts to give his daughters to them instead, but they get angry at him. The angels blind the men and take Lot with his family out of the city, and God then destroys the city. This story gets referenced in several more places in the bible.

The second is in Leviticus, where it is mentioned in two parts that are related to each other (chapters 18 and 20). Moses gives the Israelites a list of sins which they must not do if they wish to remain in the Promised Land, and that the people they were driving out in front of them were being driven out because they did these sins. Among this list it is mentioned that if a man lies with a man as he does with a woman, then the man shall be put to death.

The fourth one is in the New Testament, in the first letter to the Corinthians (chapter 6), Paul gives a list of sins that they must not do if they wish to be in the kingdom of God and that some of them were doing these things before they received the faith. Among the list it is mentioned that homosexuals shall not inherit the kingdom of God.

The fifth one is in the letter of Jude, where it briefly mentions the sin of Sodom and their lust for 'strange flesh'.

The third is the most interesting one to me as far as this book is concerned. Paul writes in the first chapter of his letter to the Romans about the sins that were taking place in Rome. He starts by talking about how the Romans could know God, but they instead chose to worship idols, and then he says that they exchanged natural relations between men and women with unnatural ones, burning in lust for each other and doing shameful things; first the women, and then the men. Then he lists a large number of other sins being committed in Rome following this.

The reason it is interesting to me is because there is actually a very profound connection between idolatry and homosexuality.

It may not be obvious, but allow me to explain this:

In the bible, the final salvation spoken of in revelations says that the Bridegroom shall come and marry the Bride. In many parts of the bible, there are references to this. The Song of Songs is often interpreted as referring to this event. Jesus in His parables about people being invited to a wedding is talking about this event.

The Bridegroom is God and the Bride is the Church. The two marry each other in the end and that is heaven; that is salvation. The priest must be a man because he is in the place of the bridegroom; Mary and other women sharing her type of role must be women because they are in the place of the bride.

It is a heterosexual union. Even males in the church, even the males who are in the place of the Bridegroom, they also count as the Bride. It is a marriage that is being consummated every time the Eucharist is performed and the body of the Bridegroom enters into the recipient of Holy Communion, just as a man's body enters his wife's body to consummate the marriage.

Human beings were created to be heterosexual because they in their own nature are a copy of this divine mystery. In a marriage, the man and his wife become one flesh; they become one. When God marries the church, when people receive the Eucharist, they are becoming one flesh with God and they are becoming God with Him.

Men and women are both made in God's image, reflecting this divine marriage through their own feminine or masculine natures.

Caiaphas was enraged with Jesus when He answered the question by declaring that He was who Caiaphas said He was, and that furthermore they would see a human being sit at the right hand of God and coming on the clouds of heaven.

Prior to Jesus' coming, who understood God's revelation like this?

What new innovation to the faith was this?

Where in the Old Testament, as they had always understood it to be, did the prophets say that a human being would share God's divinity with Him? Who among all the elders and teachers of Israel taught that a human being born of a woman was going to sit next to God as His equal? It was blasphemy, they thought, and so Caiaphas tore his clothes, something Moses did not allow the High priest to do, and said that there was no more need of witnesses, for everyone had heard what He had said.

The revelation from God did not change. The teaching did not change. Jesus was not contradicting what had been said before, despite all appearances to the contrary; it was the mistaken understanding of human beings that led them to think that He had.

Three hundred years later, in the time after Constantine granted toleration to Christianity in his empire, many people insisted that Caiaphas' understanding of the scriptural truth was the right one, and that the Messiah could not possibly have been God. The Arian heresy spread everywhere and many great saints of the time took up the task of standing against it. Athanasius of Alexandria wrote that God became man so that man could become God, and he was persecuted.

A human being really was God, and human beings were

going to become One with Him, to become God with Him through the marriage that would take place between the Bridegroom and the Bride.

Women are women and men are men, they are masculine and feminine, because they were made by an artist who painted them as a reflection of the divine mystery that all things on heaven and earth exist to fulfill.

The man takes a wife, his body enters hers, and they become one flesh together; an action repeated again and again throughout history, as an artistic allegory to the marriage between God and human beings. Jesus told the crowds that unless you eat His flesh and drink His blood you cannot have eternal life; similarly, without the man's body entering the woman's in the sexual act, a marriage can also never be consummated or truly be a marriage.

The Old Testament hinted at these things, it is true, but in no place was it ever explained like this to people. Those who already hated Jesus out of envy thus used these words of His, treating it at odds with what had been said before, and declared Him as being against God's revelation.

Jesus taught that those who do not believe in Him shall be condemned in the end. The Jews in the Old Testament taught that idols were abominable to God and that those who worshipped them would be condemned. Paul repeats in the same part in the letter to the Corinthians quoted above that those who worship idols also cannot inherit eternal life.

What does it mean to worship an idol?

As Paul said in Romans, it is to worship the creature rather than the Creator. The idolater is choosing to abandon the Truth and worship things that he is able by his reason to know are not true, because he is tempted to do so.

The society around him perhaps tells him to worship these things, and if he doesn't perhaps there are consequences to him. He perhaps does not want to believe in the Truth about his own sins and so he prefers to believe in gods who not only approve of the evil he does, but they do these evil things themselves as well. He perhaps dislikes the people who follow the true faith, or is under social pressure to stay with the religion he was raised with, or any other thing like this that prevents him from coming to the Truth that he needs to believe in order to be saved.

The sin of idolatry is the sin of abandoning the uncreated Truth in favour of things that were created.

People can see through reason that God is not like this, but He is rather like that, but they choose not to follow reason, and instead they follow what other people tell them, what the society says, what best suits their own desires, etc.

Idolatry does not just mean to worship statues as gods. It honestly has little to do with the question of whether it is statues, or whether it is polytheistic or monotheistic.

A person who has no statues and who believes in a monotheistic worldview, but who abandons the Truth in favour of believing what the world tells him about God and what he wants to believe about God, as opposed to what reason would tell him about God and what God has actually revealed about Himself, is ultimately committing the same sin as the man who worships statues he makes as gods. The sin of idolatry is the rejection of Truth in favour of created things.

A Muslim or a protestant can be just as much an idolater as the people who Paul was actually referring to who worshipped statues, because if they reject truth and abandon the pursuit of it in favour of following what their upbringing told them and what they prefer to believe, then they are essentially doing little different from the person who honours a statue as god.

They create their own god, even a monotheistic god, according to their own wishes and decisions, and not according to how He actually revealed Himself, then they are also following something that was made by human hands.

'Idolatry' is not a question of polytheism vs.

monotheism, statues vs. a formless God, but rather idolatry is a question of whether people are living in the Truth or not.

God is not angry at the person who worshipped Ba'al because it is polytheistic and it is a statue, but He is angry because the person is not living in the Truth that he can come to know through reason, had he not been held back by sin. This is what idolatry really is.

Every religion outside the catholic faith can be idolatrous if they are not living in the Truth that they can see through reason, and many Catholics inside the church can also be idolatrous if they also do not live in the Truth and prefer their own ideas over what God tells them through the gospel.

Anyone who puts something that they created themselves in place of God is committing idolatry. The person who follows Jesus Christ and yet who decides himself who Jesus Christ is (even if the person is a catholic), rather than listening to the church, is also an idolater, because he is essentially making his own god with his own hands.

On the other hand, there can be people who do believe in a pantheon of false gods, but who reject all the irrational myths said about these gods and believe that the truth about the powers in the heavens is something more than this which they have been taught, but they admit in honesty that they do not know what that is. And this person is not an idolater, because he is following God as He reveals Himself through nature to the best of his ability and is not creating his own god.

Rather than following the Truth, who is God, people follow the creation instead, they follow the people around them instead, they follow their own desires instead, and believe in God as they want Him to be and not as He truly reveals Himself to be. And thus, they serve the creature rather than the Creator.

Such people can be worshippers of Zeus or Apollo, they can also be Buddhists, Hindus, Muslims, Sikhs, protestants, Orthodox and even Catholics. God is not angry at idolaters because of the presence of an image but rather because they are not following Him, and they are deciding for themselves who He is, according to what they desire to believe.

They seek salvation, not from God, at least not God as He really is, but rather in the God or gods or truths that they believe in His place.

The truth that God has revealed in the world is contained within the gospel of Jesus Christ. The correct teaching of the gospel of Jesus Christ is guaranteed only within the Catholic Church, and all other churches are subject to error. But many people do not follow the Catholic Church and they follow other religions, not because God has guided them there, but because created persons and created things have directed them in the wrong direction. They perhaps were born in these religions and their parents or society taught them it was true, and so they believed it; but it was because of the creature, not the Creator, they were kept away from the Truth.

If people can find salvation with created things, and without God, then this is like saying the Bride can marry the Bride, or as Paul says that their women gave up natural relations with men. If God can be contented with leaving human beings seeking their salvation from created things and without Him, it is like saying that the Bridegroom can marry the Bridegroom; and so, as Paul says that after the women gave up natural relations, so the men gave up natural relations with women and burned with lust for one another.

To be able to find salvation in some alternative way than the Bridegroom marrying the Bride is akin to saying that people can marry in a way different than the heterosexual relationship.

Human beings were designed for God, and God desired human beings. Human beings exchanged their natural relations with God, for unnatural relations with idols. And they followed gods who did not offer human beings the opportunity to become one with them, but were content to be gods without human beings joining them, like how the men burned in lust for one another. The unnatural lust was just a reflection of the unnatural spiritual reality surrounding them.

There is a truly profound connection between the sin of human beings in looking for salvation without the true God and homosexuality. There is a profound connection between the teaching on homosexuality and the teaching on salvation outside of the church.

The church for many centuries always taught that salvation outside the church was impossible. Similarly, for many centuries, it has also taught that homosexual relations can never be accepted in God's plan. These two teachings are both part of the same mystery.

In fact, all the teachings on marriage are linked to this mystery of salvation. It is not the case that every heterosexual act is licit, similarly it is not the case that everyone who seeks salvation in the church is going to find it either. Many people have heterosexual relations in ways that are not permitted and which do not constitute a true marriage; similarly, many people seek salvation from Jesus, but not from within the church. Many people have heterosexual relations that are true marriages, but they sin within the marriage; many Catholics, even though they be living in the true marriage with God, are not going to find salvation.

These two mysteries are deeply connected with one another.

Can this teaching change? If it can change, then it is not from God.

It is possible for the understanding of human beings of the gospel can change, but it is not possible that the gospel can change.

With regard to the teaching on no salvation outside of the church, the understanding of this teaching has changed very drastically over the centuries.

In the Council of Basel-Ferrara-Florence (held in the 15th century) there was a decree in it from the later sessions, which read:

It firmly believes, professes and preaches that all those who are outside the catholic church, not only pagans but also Jews or heretics and schismatics, cannot share in eternal life and will go into the everlasting fire which was prepared for the devil and his angels, unless they are joined to the catholic church before the end of their lives; that the unity of the ecclesiastical body is of such importance that only for those who abide in it do the church's sacraments contribute to salvation and do fasts, almsgiving and other works of piety and practices of the Christian militia produce eternal rewards; and that nobody can be saved, no matter how much he has given away in alms and even if he has shed his blood in the name of Christ, unless he has persevered in the bosom and the unity of the catholic church.

Alongside this quotation from the council, let us here place a quotation from the catechism used in the church today (published in the 1990s):

1260 "Since Christ died for all, and since all men are in fact called to one and the same destiny, which is divine, we must hold that the Holy Spirit offers to all the possibility of being made partakers, in a way known to God, of the Paschal mystery." Every man who is ignorant of the Gospel of Christ and of his Church, but seeks the truth and does the will of God in accordance with his understanding of it, can be saved. It may be supposed that such persons would have desired Baptism explicitly if they had known its necessity.

The gospel has not changed, but the way that the bishops and relevant authorities have taught about it has changed very greatly on this point. The statement from the 15th century essentially states that every single person outside of the church, even if they die a martyr in the name of Christ, will all go to hell unless they become Catholic before their deaths.

The statement from the 20th century states that if someone outside of the church is innocently ignorant of the gospel, then he may find salvation by following God in his own way.

These two statements are both authoritative, although the former more than the latter, because ecumenical councils have more weight than catechisms (the Second Vatican Council, which is an ecumenical council, has similarly statements as the catechism on the question, however). Both have come from the magisterium and the Spirit that inspires it. But when putting them together, they must be interpreted in a way that is not contradictory.

This can only be done if we understand it like this: all people outside the church will go to hell, no matter what religion or faith they hold, unless they are seeking the truth and doing what they know is right, in which case they are counted as people seeking salvation in the church, without which people cannot be saved.

This understanding that the church (speaking of its membership) has today is not the same understanding that it had centuries ago. How many saints were there who taught that all who died in other religions were doomed to hell? How many bishops and Popes said such? A hundred years ago, if the question was put to the Vatican if Confucius or Socrates could have been considered saved, the response may have been in the negative.

But if that is true, then that means that there are people living in other religions, in other faiths, who are seeking after the Creator when in fact they appear like they are worshipping what was created by human beings. And even though they may die in other faiths, they will still get to heaven, because they are not really in other faiths, because they believe that the Truth is more than just what they have presented with in their various faiths, but they just have not met a person who showed to them what this Truth was.

There is no one who dies and goes to heaven except in the catholic faith. What the council said cannot be undone.

However, God created every person in the world with a desire for Him, and it can be assumed that a person who isn't living in sin, in fact does desire Him, even though He doesn't know who He is, because God created every human being with such a desire. It is the natural state of the human being to desire God.

If a catechumen dies before baptism, he is not considered damned for that reason. But, when exactly does Catechism start? Does it begin when the person first enters the church, or does it begin when the person first hears the Truth?

A person who never hears about God, but who believes what the angels sent by God reveal through nature and follows it in his life… is he not also accepting catechism? If he dies before a missionary comes, is he not also a catechumen who dies before baptism?

People in other religions who are living in the Truth are just catechumens prior to baptism that have not yet heard preaching yet. Every person begins life as a catechumen; the human being was designed to be God's student. But, it is those people who reject the Truth that God teaches them (whether through nature or through preaching or other means), because of so many obstacles placed in their way, who cannot be saved.

I am not sure if this makes too much sense, so I thought I may give some examples to think about:

A boy is born in India to a Hindu family. His parents raise him as a Hindu and he goes to the temple from time to time to give his worship to various Hindu gods. However, there are many things he is told that he finds far-fetched and doesn't believe them. He looks for evidence to know if these gods are true and doesn't find it. He believes that there is an intelligent design behind the world, but is not sure whether all that he is told is true and keeps looking and questioning. He is being honest with himself and honest to other people. He is not sure what the Truth is, but he is open to it.

This person is not living in idolatry. His search for the Truth is a search for the Catholic faith, because he was designed for the Catholic faith, but he just doesn' t know it.

His parents and relatives try to sway him and make him to accept the things they accept, to believe the things they believe, but he resists them and stays within his search for the truth. Thus, he is enduring as a catechumen to the Catholic faith and not being swayed aside to worshipping what humans made themselves. He satisfies what the council asks for as a person who endures in the Catholic faith, because his search for Truth is a search for the Catholic faith.

And God shows Him things about Himself. He believes in God' s moral law as he sees it revealed in nature and follows it in his life. He believes that God is loving, God is good, and He can trust God, even though he mistakenly thinks that God is a pantheon of many gods.

He was born a catechumen, and God is his Teacher, silently teaching him throughout his life as he searches for a Truth he doesn' t know.

If he had gone astray from this and followed what his parents had pushed him towards, followed what others pushed him towards, as opposed to being honest with himself and following the Truth that he knew, then he could not be saved because he was leaving his catechesis from God in order to follow something made by human hands.

He is saved through the catholic faith, and not through

Hinduism, but God uses his upbringing and his environment to teach him things about Himself and this person follows those things in his life.

He is not following a god that was created, but a God who reveals Himself to him.

Another boy, born in England to Anglican parents is raised as an Anglican. He takes a great interest in religion and becomes an Anglican priest and after a career, he becomes an Anglican bishop. He often finds things in the bible that seem contradictory to him and he often finds himself unsure about what the bible means.

He comes across all kinds of internal discrepancies in what his religion believes, but rather than be honest and admit to them, he washes them over and does not confront them with sincerity. He uses sophistry to defend certain things he believes and to reject things he doesn't believe; but his arguments contradict each other and if they were all laid out, they would not add up to something logical.

This bishop regularly attends interfaith meetings and ecumenical prayers. He has even met the Pope and is a friend of his. He encourages dialogue and cooperation between the churches.

He does not want to admit that there are any problems in his beliefs, because that will make him question his entire life, it will perhaps provoke scandal among those around him, he may not be able to continue to be bishop anymore, and thus he resists the voice that tells him to be sincere and instead holds firm on what he outwardly seems to believe.

The Pope and the catholic bishops, unwittingly assist him in this by telling him that there is no need for him to convert or to reject the religion his parents gave to him, because someone in his religion can be saved too.

And so, he dies and goes to hell, because God was trying to speak to him through all those doubts and to get himself to live in the Truth, and yet he resisted it and deceived many others who followed what he taught, because he preferred the world over the Truth.

As far as other religions are concerned, it is often the clergy and not the laity, who have the greatest guilt in the question of failing to find the Truth, because more knowledge was given to them and yet they continued to serve as clergy in their faiths.

Another man, a Muslim in a poor village in northern Nigeria, cannot read or write and what he knows about his Islamic faith is quite small in comparison with someone who has a clerical status.

Thus, unlike the bishop, he is not filled with doubts

about his religion, because he doesn't actually know what his religion teaches. He knows that God exists and thinks that Muhammad is his messenger, but he can't read the Quran himself. He sees Muslims doing evil things, even doing evil things in the name of God, and he thinks that such things must not have been allowed in the Quran, without knowing what the Quran actually said.

Even things which the evildoers in question can actually prove through scriptures are things that Muhammad commanded, he will assume that these things are against Islam because they are evil. He believes that God is a loving God, a just God, a good God, and that He does not want Muslims to fight people like this or to do things that are bad.

He believes that God is so good and loving that God would do anything out of love for human beings. He thinks that God would even sacrifice Himself out of love for human beings, and assumes that the Quran must say something about this in support of it.

And whenever pressures are put on him to believe in another version of the Quran, one which is truer to the text, he rejects it and insists that this is not who God is.

He is living with sincerity. He is living in the Truth. He is following what God is showing him through the law written on his heart. Like all human beings, he was born a catechumen and is following the instruction that God gives to him in his life, but just doesn't understand that what he calls the 'Quran' is really something else.

He endures in the Catholic faith, by rejecting the God that human beings create and instead following God as He truly reveals Himself: through nature, through reason, through many ways within the environment he was raised in.

If he had followed what the clerics had taught and not what he knew was true, then he would be an idolater and he could not find salvation, because he is following a created God and not God as He truly is. He is saved because He believes in the God of the Truth and not in the God of the Quran, even though he mistakenly believes that the God he believes in is the God of the Quran.

An atheist in China owns a business and lives as she likes to live. She mistreats her workers, breaks the law when she can get away with it, bribes officials, and treats other people as something lower than her.

She has no time for God or religious questions, because she thinks that all that matters is making money and being successful.

She gets angry when other people are unfair to her, and meanwhile she is unfair to everyone.

And she is not happy. She hoards wealth only to make

more wealth and never feels contented no matter how much she spends on herself.

Although she is not happy, she doesn't think there is anything else that can satisfy her. She sees people going after spiritual things, and she thinks they are stupid and are wasting time. She is too arrogant to accept that they know things that she doesn't.

She is not honest with herself, however. Because she knows she is not happy the way she lives but she doesn't admit to it. She sees spiritual people who seem to be more content than she is, and yet she doesn't want to think it is true, because she is too proud to stop thinking like she is wiser than them.

These spiritual people around her, some of them Christians, some of them Buddhists, some of them other things, seem to be better people than she is, but she doesn't want to believe this so she refuses to admit to it and let go of her pride.

And so, she dies and goes down to hell, because although she and all human beings were created as catechumens, she didn't listen to the voice of the Teacher in her life and instead insisted on following her own ideas in His place. And thus, for her idolatry she is condemned.

Another atheist, living in England, lives a very moral life and thinks that all people should be treated with respect and dignity. She thinks that people ought to live for helping others and she tries to live like this in her own life.

She loves people of religion and treats them with respect. She is not like other atheists she knows, and thinks it is wrong to mock people of religion for their beliefs.

She accepts the possibility that religion may be true, but she just honestly admits that she hasn't seen anything that has shown her that religion was true.

Rather than believing in religion, she believes in Truth and believes that Truth controls all things in the universe and people ought to live according to the Truth. She thinks that if people live according to the Truth, then they will all live trying to help other people, like how she tries to live.

She does not think that she is better than others; she admits she has imperfections like others do, but has never met a person of religion that seemed to her like he was a better person than her.

There are many pressures in her life that try to convince her that it is better to live selfishly, but she resists this and holds on the Truth that she lives by, which teaches her that she ought to love other people.

She does not have much contact with real believers in

religion, and most of those she knows seem to her to just follow the various religions they follow because that was how they were raised and they themselves do not live by what they believe in any really serious way.

She dies and sees God; He shows to her that He loves her and wants to be with her, and she feels delighted to know that He is real and that He was the Truth that she followed in her life.

Every person is a catechumen from the time they are born, and God is teaching all of them, but not everyone follows Him, and many prefer to follow what human beings create instead. If one can follow God by believing Him to be many gods rather than one God, then one can also follow God by calling Him Truth and without realizing He was a person at all.

A cradle Catholic in the United States is raised in the faith by his parents, but he doesn't like to follow its teachings. He thinks the church needs to change and adapt itself to the modern world, because there are too many things they restrict and do not allow people to have.

He doesn't want to leave the church, because he feels like the church is his home and he wants the church to change so that he can feel more at home within it. He dislikes converts who enter the church from other faiths and who hold to the teachings of the church even more than he does, because he thinks that he was born a Catholic and these people are intruding into his home.

He says that the church is out of touch with the modern world, and that there are so many good people outside the church who live fine without following the church's teachings. He supports prelates and priests who reject what the church teaches and calls them progressive, and dislikes those who hold firm to teaching and calls them traditionalist.

He does not follow the church's teachings in his life, and he receives communion every week, because he thinks that this belongs to him since he was born in the church.

Rather than following the church's teachings, he instead follows an idea of good that is promoted by the popular culture he lives in, but which is at odds with the church's traditions. He openly violates the church teaching in many ways, believes that the church is wrong and receives the Eucharist. He thinks that the real Jesus is different from what the church says.

This person dies and sees Jesus, but Jesus tells him, 'I was standing in front of you the whole time within the teachings you rejected, and you kept rejecting me in favour of the world', and he departs from Jesus into the eternal darkness.

This man is also committing a kind of idolatry, because he does not follow Jesus as He actually is, but instead follows the Jesus he created with his own mind. And so, he also is following the creature rather than the Creator, and is doomed to hellfire.

Consider even particular historical figures within pagan cultures who were seeking the Truth, at least in appearances.

Socrates claimed that the gods of the Greeks could not possibly really be the way the myths presented them and he believed that the Truth was something different from this. He taught that human beings could only be free if they didn't follow their bodily desires. He was forced to drink hemlock for not agreeing to what the people of Athens thought was true, and he died like a martyr to a God he didn't know, in a place where Paul would later come to proclaim the unknown god to the people who lived there.

The 12th century Indian philosopher Basava disagreed with the beliefs of Hindus that people were born into lower or upper castes, and said that people were equal regardless of gender, class or caste. He tried to reform the society of his day. He was devoted to Shiva, but he didn't believe the same things as other Hindus believed; he rejected the idols. One of his famous poems about

Shiva (lord of the meeting rivers) is translated as follows (this and the second quote, from wikipedia article: https://en.wikipedia.org/wiki/Basava) :

How can I feel right
    about a god who eats up lacquer and melts,
        who wilts when he sees fire?

How can I feel right
    about gods you sell in your need,
        and gods you bury for fear of thieves?

The lord of the meeting rivers,
self-born, one with himself,
he alone is the true god.

His followers put his teachings into practice and this brought scandal. When a Brahmin girl was going to get married to a lower caste boy, the king was so enraged that the boy and the girl were dragged through the streets to die and the people attending the wedding had their eyes gouged out. Basava tried to stop his followers from using violence against the king, but they didn't listen. He died shortly afterwards. He didn't know the gospel, but he appeared to be following it in his life.

Before he died, one of his last musings was about how the gods favoured the rich because they could build more temples than the poor, so they could get greater favour than the poor. But he said that the temple of the body itself would suffice just as well as the temples built by the rich; that ultimately God was more interested in the human being himself than with the wealth possessed. And he wrote this poem:

The rich
will make temples for Shiva,
What shall I,
a poor man do?

My legs are pillars,
the body the shrine,
the head a cupola of gold.

Listen, O lord of the meeting rivers,
things standing shall fall,
but the moving ever shall stay.

Gandhi was never baptized, but is it difficult to say that he was following the gospel in his life? His teachings about non-violence, about self-sacrifice for others, about love for the poor, about putting aside hatred and forgiveness; is it possible he was following God when he was doing these things? And he also died like a martyr at the hands of a Hindu extremist who rejected what he had done.

Gandhi wrote, 'God is Truth, and the way to Truth is by ahimsa (non-violence)'.

Confucius never heard of the God of Israel, but his

teachings about how people ought to live in this world
were honoured by Catholic missionaries like Matteo
Ricci who came to China. The Chinese name for God
 'tianzhu' (天主)，means master of heaven, and it
itself came from the inspiration of Chinese texts. Heaven
was the highest of all places and a master was the
highest of positions. The Confucians claimed that the
wife must obey the husband, the man must obey his
master, the master must obey the state, the state must
obey the king, and the king must obey heaven. And like
Paul in Athens, Matteo Ricci told the Chinese that the
'master of heaven' (ie. the one who ruled heaven) was
the God he was now proclaiming to them.

Human beings finding salvation from created things, is a
gay marriage in the spiritual sense.

When people are going after the creature rather than
the Creator, it is like homosexuality. In my examples
above, the Anglican bishop, the atheist in China, the
cradle catholic that rejects the church's teachings–
they are like homosexuals in a spiritual sense, because
they were trying to find their salvation from something
created, rather than the Creator Himself.

God's heart desired His Spouse. Jesus was in agony in
the garden because He was in misery without His bride,
like the sinner in hell forever barred from the sight of

God. A rib was taken from Adam to give life to his wife, and so a spear was put into the rib of Christ, and the water and blood that came out was what gave life to the church.

God created woman to be a companion to man because it was not good for the man to be alone. The Trinity created human beings because they saw it was not good for them to be alone.

The Trinity desires the church, and the church needs the Trinity for its salvation; it is a heterosexual relationship.

In 1 Corinthians 6, Paul says that those who commit idolatry cannot inherit eternal life. The bible says that all who call on the name of the Lord shall be saved.

God does not want people to go to hell. He desperately wants people to find salvation; it was for that reason that He died on the cross. How can it be that someone could think that the God who suffered this much for human beings for their salvation would meet a Jew, an atheist, a pagan or a protestant upon their death, and tell them that He doesn't want them, because they never knew what the whole Truth was even though they were sincerely living in it?

A catechumen who dies before baptism is considered as one who died within the bosom and unity of the church, even though he has not yet received the sacrament that joins him to Christ's body.

But when does a person first become a catechumen? Is it when they first hear a missionary preach to them, or is it when they first hear the Truth?

Like Abraham interceding with God over Sodom, we can do something similar here,

'If the person dies the day before he is baptized, but he was going to get baptized if given enough time, will God reject him, because he was short of one day?'

He will not reject him, for being short of one day.

'If the person dies two months before he is baptized, but he was going to get baptized if given two more months, will God reject him, because he was short of two months?

He will not reject him, for being short of two months

'If the person dies a year before being baptized, and has not yet fully understood many of the church's teachings, but was still working on many of the concepts. He does not quite know what the Trinity is and why Jesus came down to the world. But if given another year, he would understand it all and get baptized. Will God reject him, because he was short of one year?'

He will not reject him, for being short of one year

'If the person has not yet entered the catechism class,

but he is contemplating on contacting the Catholic church because he is thinking of possibly becoming a Catholic because he senses that it is teaching the truth, but needs to learn more about it. And after two more years he would have gotten baptized, but he dies then. Will God reject him, for being short of two years?'

He will not reject him, for being short of two years.

'If the person has not yet heard what the Catholic Church is, but he follows the moral teachings of the church in his life and believes that all people should live like this, and if he was given another five years, he would have encountered the Catholic Church and believed it, and gotten baptized. Will God reject him, for being short of five years?'

He will not reject him, for being short of five years

'If the person lives in a place where the Catholic Church is not going to come for another 100 years, and no one has ever heard of it there. But the Truth that comes from God is still present in the culture, because God has planted seeds, and some follow this Truth while others do not, and this person follows this Truth with all of his heart, and if he had lived another 100 years, he would have met the first missionaries and received baptism, but he dies instead. Will God reject him, for being short of one hundred years?'

He will not reject him, for being short of one hundred years.

They are all catechumens before baptism, but just different lengths of time and different degrees of understanding. God offers Himself as a teacher to every human being from the time they are born, but few listen to His voice and endure together within the Truth He presents to them in whatever culture they are raised in. Those who endure within this Truth, they are the ones who endure within the bosom and unity of church, because God is the Spouse of the church and those who endure with Him are enduring with the church, but those who seek after created things instead of Him, they are the ones who follow idols and will be condemned.

These are people who are looking for the Truth; if given enough time, they would find it eventually and get baptized into it, and God will not throw them away just because they expired before baptism. The people who go to hell are those who are not looking for the Truth, who would not find it no matter how much time you gave to them because their problem is not only just ignorance; even if the missionary came and taught them, they still would not believe.

At the end of Mark's gospel, Jesus says, 'Those who believe and are baptized will be saved, and those who do not believe will be condemned'. Pay attention, He does not say 'Those who believe and are baptized will be saved, and those who do not believe or are not baptized shall be condemned', but rather He says only that those who do not believe will be condemned. And I think this must be deliberate.

I feel like the Lord deliberately says that it is only lack of belief rather than lack of baptism that condemns a person to hell; implying that a person who is not baptized, but believes, is not heading to hell or at least not hell in the eternal sense. If He didn't intend this, then why didn't He say 'not believe or not baptized', when in the first sentence He did state that both were necessary for salvation?

Baptism is necessary for salvation, but He is not going to condemn someone who believes and is not yet baptized. Somehow the person will receive baptism, even if they seemingly die without it.

With regard to the quote from the Council I presented before. We must believe it and accept it, but we do not need to interpret it the same way as it was understood by the people who wrote it.

Ultimately, in facing church teaching, we must also decide whether we are following the bishops who speak it or we are following the Person who speaks through them.

If it is the creature (the bishops) we follow, then we ought to follow their interpretation according to what they thought it meant, but if it is the Person who speaks through them we follow, then we ought to interpret it under the light of the Sacred Heart.

The bible contains the entirety of what God wishes to say to the world, but the bible needs the authority of the church to be interpreted correctly; like what the Ethiopian said to Philip when reading Isaiah- he needed the apostle's help to understand what was being said. And the teachings of the church cannot be correctly understood without being put under the light of the Sacred Heart.

Keep in mind, and this is very important. No one goes to heaven as a Jew, a Buddhist, a Muslim, an atheist, etc. All enter heaven as Catholics only. For those of them that are following the Truth sincerely it is just that they haven't yet fully understood the Truth that they were following in their lives and that this Truth is the Catholic faith.

And anyone who resists this call to become a Catholic to follow what they want to follow instead, cannot be saved.

Even if the Pope or bishops tell them they do not need to convert, they still cannot be saved, because it is not by the creature (the bishops) that one finds salvation, but by the Creator.

The council remains completely true: such people are still going to heaven through endurance in the Catholic faith and not through their own religions.

Why did the church understand this differently before?

Allow me to present something for you to imagine.

When Christ was on the Cross and He was suffering out of love for humanity, for a humanity that didn't believe in God's love, could you imagine it like this:

Christ is on the cross, gazing at the people around Him, including the Jews and Roman soldiers, and with bloodshot eyes, He grinds His teeth in anger and yells out in hatred, 'And whoever doesn't believe I am God and get baptized, whether they are Jews or pagans or heretics, all will go to hell and burn forever!'

What do you think, was it like this?

The truth is that the number of people in the world who think of some variant of God like this is not small in number, although perhaps they would never believe Christ was like this on the cross.

Now, Jesus did, however, say in the gospel of John that He who does not believe that I am He will perish in their sins. He did, however, say that He who calls Him Lord, Lord and does not do what He tells Him will not be recognized by Him at the last day and will not find salvation. At the end of Mark's gospel, Jesus says that whoever does not believe will be condemned.

But this is not quite the same as the way I just wrote above. The doctrine seems the same whether it be the example I just wrote or what Jesus actually said in John's gospel, but the Heart, the Mind, the intention-these things do not look the same.

The end meaning, being that those without faith in Jesus are going to find hellfire, is still the same whether we compare my example with what was actually written in the gospel, but you could come away with two completely ideas of who God was and what was in His Heart on the basis of whether you followed my example or what the gospel actually said.

The difference is actually very important, because Jesus in fact died on the cross to prove to people that God's love was real. And He resurrected from the dead to prove to people that it was God, and not just a human being, who had this love.

If the church doesn＇t believe in God＇s love, then none of these doctrines have any purpose in them, because they are completely grounded within the belief that they are from a God who is all-loving for all His creatures. Like trying to understand Newtonian physics without even knowing basic mathematics, a person can never correctly understand Catholic doctrine without understanding the Person behind it.

No one goes to hell because God wants them there. They go to hell because they reject God, not because He rejects them. He will do anything He can to bring people to heaven. The people outside the church cannot find salvation, because the church is salvation and **they** do not want it; it is not that God doesn't want them.

Those who do want it, but just don＇t realize that they want it, although they would realize it had they been given more time– how could anyone possibly believe that God would reject them? Only those who fail to understand how much He suffered on the cross for His beloved could ever think like this.

Do you follow the law or the Spirit? Do you follow the written texts or the Person behind the texts who is speaking through them?

Imagine a workplace where the boss gives an order to people, but the situation changes while the boss is not present such that the order no longer seems to make sense. Some of the employees insist that they must do what the boss says, while the others insist that they must do what the boss would want them to do in this situation. They argue with one another, and those who insist that they should follow what he said, abusively push out the other employees and treat them badly. The two groups split up, and they carry out what they think is right according to their own understanding, one doing what the boss said and the other doing what they think the boss would want them to do. The boss then returns and sees what has happened and he is very angry with those who did what he said and not what he wanted. He tells them, 'How could you not know that I would want you to change the plan when the circumstances changed like this?' and the employees answer him, 'but you cannot blame us, because we did as you say.' And the boss rejects them and gives bonuses to the other employees, while he fires the first group.

This was the error of the Scribes and the Pharisees, this was the error of the Jews that were condemned in Paul's letters, who held to the written law without the

Spirit, or in other words who followed what was written on the page without understanding the desires of the Person behind what was written on the page. Many Christians have committed this same error in history and continue to do so today, in that they follow the law and not the Spirit; they look at the text and forget the Person that made the text have any meaning in the first place.

It is partly for this reason that the devotion to the Sacred Heart is so important for the church. Because without contemplating the heart of God, and the gospel that came from it, it is impossible to correctly understand any of the inspired doctrines that have come from the church's understanding of the gospel.

Lord, we pray that you help us to understand and love the Person who stands behind all of the doctrines of the Church. Help us to always understand Church teaching under the light He provides and according to His Sacred Heart. We ask for these things, if it is your will, in Jesus' name, Amen

II: Sexual Sins

Today, a huge number of people in western countries as well as growing numbers in other parts of the world, question whether the traditional condemnations their societies attached to homosexuality were really warranted. More and more people ask the question as to why it is if two men or two women want to have a sexual relationship with each other, who is being harmed by it?

And a lot of Catholics do not understand why the church teaches this either.

Who exactly is the victim of a sexual sin?

Without a victim there is no sin, and there can be no punishment either.

And the church, the bible, and in fact most religions teach that there are sinful ways of using the gift of sexuality, but the question is who is hurt by using sex in a way outside of marriage?

In the case of rape or adultery, it is rather obvious who is hurt.

However, the church goes so much further than that. It tells us that masturbation is wrong, that pornography is wrong, that sex before marriage is wrong, that divorce and remarriage is wrong, that sex in a way closed to procreation is wrong, and therefore of course that sex between members of the same sex is wrong.

But in many of these acts, the victim is not so obvious. Who are you hurting if you are not married and masturbate? How are you victimizing someone if you have a sexual relationship with someone of the same sex who you want to spend your life with?

Suppose that the individuals involved in these acts do not mean to harm either themselves or others, and in fact they genuinely care about themselves and others. So, where is the sin? Where are they hurting someone and creating a victim by what they do?

It is so hard for many people to see where the victim is, and yet all across the world throughout history, in every culture, the taboos and moral condemnations surrounding an improper use of sexuality can be found almost everywhere.

On a psychological level, or on an evolutionary level, societies perhaps have found some benefits to their survival in placing such taboos or restrictions on how human sexuality can express itself. But, if put to the test of reason, unless there is someone who is actually victimized by these sexual acts, then there are no grounds for calling them sinful.

Now, where is the victim? Even if everyone in the world felt no offense or injury at a particular sinful sexual act being committed, God Himself feels offense and hurt over it. Hence, God is the victim of the act.

But why would God be a victim? Why does it matter to Him how human beings use their sexuality?

God loves human beings more than their mother and father, more than their children, more than their closest friend or their most intimate spouse. Every single thing that a human being does, says or thinks, matters a lot to God. He is an extremely sensitive Person, and everything that you do, say or think, will affect Him.

God gave many gifts to the human being, and gave him many different faculties in his being. He created the human being in His own image and likeness, and He designed the human being for Himself.

The entire universe was made as the stage in which human beings and God would get married – when human beings and God would become One in heaven. Nothing exists which is not related to this purpose. And God gave human beings the gift of sexuality as a reflection of this marriage in heaven.

Men and women marry one another, because it reflects how God marries the church. The physical marriage on earth is the copy, and the marriage in heaven is the original.

Just as the deepest part of all things is this marriage in heaven, so also the deepest part of the human being is touched by his sexuality.

He designed us like this, because He was painting a picture. Human sexuality on Earth is a reflection of the mystery of salvation between God and human beings.

Every aspect of human sexuality is included within this. I have already mentioned that homosexuality is like a reflection of the seeking of the creature rather than the Creator.

The person who divorces his wife and marries another,

is like the person who leaves the church to join a schismatic church. She has left her husband for another one, like how the believer leaves their first husband and finds another one, changes one church for another one in schism with it, to marry one who can never be her true husband.

If it is permissible for human beings to leave their spouse and marry another, then it must also be OK for schismatic churches to exist.

The person who masturbates is like the person who seeks after salvation without faith. The person wants sexuality without a spouse, like how a person wants to be happy without God.

The person who commits adultery within a marriage is like the person who goes to church and also goes to another religion at the same time. She has a husband, but she is spending time with another man at the same time, like how a believer goes to church and worships another god at the same time.

The person who has sex prior to the legal marriage is like the one who receives the Eucharist before receiving baptism or entering the church. She plans to marry her boyfriend, but has not done so yet, and is having sex even though it has not yet been legally formalized. Similarly, the person comes to a Catholic church and the body of God enters her, even though she has not yet legally been admitted to the sacrament.

The person who has sex with a prostitute is like the person who follows religion on the basis of the goods of this world and not on the basis of faith. They are only together because he is using her for something, and she is using him for something. Similarly, there are people who follow one religion or another, not because they are seeking God, but because they are seeking the goods of the world.

Every sexual feeling, sexual act and sexual identity of anyone anywhere is a reflection of this mystery. God created people in a particular way, and designed them for marriage, and the way He created them was good, but they took this gift and abused it in so many ways. God created all people to believe and worship Him, but they sinned in so many ways against it.

The myriad of ways that people have sexual feelings all reflect different natures of this union between God and human beings.

There are people who enjoy being submissive slaves in sex or being dominant masters/mistresses in sex. Similarly, God came down to the Earth to be a slave to His spouse, so that she would someday love Him back and become a slave to Him.

There are men who enjoy wearing women' s clothing in sex with women. God came down to Earth and took the appearance of a created being in order to give salvation to creatures, He was God but He took on a human vestige, just like how the man, as a reflection of the bridegroom, takes on the clothing and vestiges of the bride when having sex with his spouse, who is reflecting the bride by her gender.

There are people who enjoy role-playing in sex with all sorts of different situations. Similarly, the people who come up for communion in mass all come from different lives and backgrounds, each in a different role when the body of God enters theirs and the marriage is consummated.

There are people who want sex in times or places it is not allowed. Similarly, God calls people to follow Him even in countries where the church is illegal, where believing will be met with opposition or social rejection. And it is in this place where they are not allowed to believe, that they find salvation, like how the man and his spouse have sex in times or places where it was against the rules.

There are people who enjoy being rough in sex. Similarly, the way that people find salvation is often not done smoothly, but involves many falls along the way.

Men often have much stronger sexual lusts than women. Similarly, God cares more about forgiving people and bringing them to salvation then they do.

Men many times in a day think about sex over and over

again, while women perhaps not as much. Similarly, God is always thinking of bringing us to salvation, far more than we human beings are.

There are men who become drag queens and make public performances, dressing and acting in ways that a normal woman would never do. Perhaps they perform even in a very sexualized manner in front of their audience. The pagans created gods that were like human beings. And yet these gods were not human beings, because they possessed forms and abilities that no normal human being ever had. These gods were in a human-like form, but not really human beings and people worshipped them. The man who becomes the drag queen, like a woman but not at all really a woman, is like the pagan god who takes on avatars and forms like the human being, but not at all like really a human being. And people worship these gods, even though they are not inviting us to become one with them in the spiritual marriage, just like how the audience watches the sexualized show of the drag queen and takes pleasure from it, even though there is no marriage.

The divine becoming human is very much like the taking on of qualities of the opposite sex. Both for good and for bad, because God Himself truly did become a human being, even though many people would corrupt God's appearance to make Him like themselves. In just the same way, a drag queen who performs like this in a manner that inspires sexual feelings is doing something evil, but the drag queen who is a drag queen with his wife only in a relationship open to life is doing something good, and his own self in this relationship with his wife in a unique way reflects the nature of the mystery of God becoming a human being to marry His spouse.

There are women who are not comfortable with being in a relationship with a man, because they can't find a male spouse who would love them like a woman could and so they go after a lesbian relationship instead. Perhaps even they suffered some kind of abuse or lack of love from men in their lives. Similarly, people leave the church and go to other religions, and thus seek after the creature, or perhaps do not come to the church in the first place, because they don't see any love in the church and the lack of love is the roadblock that prevents them from coming to their husband.

Sexuality, even when it is something good, is seen as something dirty and as though it was shameful, and not something beautiful. Similarly, Jesus Christ is persecuted and what is called by His name is rejected throughout the world.

We are like this, because God is like this. We are the

painting, and He is the painter. Every aspect of our gender and sexuality is a reflection of this mystery of the marriage in heaven. We can learn much about what the union between God and human beings is like by contemplating human sexuality.

Our sexuality is a very deep part of us and it has to be like this, because it is a reflection of the deepest mystery in the universe.

If a human being used the gift of sexuality only for their own pleasure, without sharing it with another person then this meant that the deepest part of the human being, in their deepest heart, in their deepest psychology, in the deepest part of their soul, there was only pleasure and no one else. The deepest part of who this person was has no other person that it is being shared with.

When a man has a wife, and the wife has sex with another man, he Is deeply hurt by this. If she even just flirts with another man, he may be deeply hurt by this. It hurts him, because this is his wife. He is a victim, because she matters to him.

God cares about us more than mothers do for children, more than husbands do for wives, or wives for husbands, more than children do for parents, more than any human being does for another human being.

If it hurts a man to see his wife with another man, then it hurts God even more for a human being to use their sexuality apart from Him, because He is even more sensitive to her than her husband is.

A dog whistle is a whistle that when a human blows into it, he can't hear anything, but a dog who has ears that are different from a human, can hear the whistle and if the dog is trained, he will respond to it and come to the person blowing the whistle, even though the person blowing the whistle doesn't hear anything at all.

If you can imagine this, that God actually feels pain at the sight of abuses of human sexuality, while human beings themselves feel intense pleasure in it. The human being is not able to feel the pain that God feels at the sight of it, and He feel this pain because it was His nature to feel this pain.

It was designed to be used for love, and instead it is used for pleasure, and so God feels intense pain at the sight of it, but the human being is oblivious to this pain.

It is for this reason, that among all the ways that Jesus could have been tempted, He could not have had sexual temptations, because He would only feel pain and not pleasure at the sight of abuses of sexuality, and thus they could not be alluring to Him.

It hurts Him very deeply to see the human being He loves so much to abuse how they are created like this. It hurts Him emotionally to see this.

When the human being uses the gift of sexuality for personal pleasure and without love for another person, He is their victim, even if they do not think they are hurting anyone.

If you go to many Catholic apologists, they may try to explain why different sexual habits are harmful for psychology, are harmful to the brain, or things like this. And while this may be true (I don't know), this is not really the reason why the church condemns these things. If this was the reason, then all the people who sincerely thought they were not hurting their psychology or brain (perhaps other scientists told them that is was beneficial to psychology and mental health) by engaging in these behaviours would have no sin, because they were just making a mistake and not actually knowingly victimizing someone.

While this type of argument may be good at showing how God's plan is present within the church's teaching on these things, it is not really the reason behind why these things are wrong. If in fact scientists were able to prove that masturbation under some forms was actually beneficial to mental or bodily health, it still would not be morally acceptable. It ultimately is not really a question of psychology or health.

Now, sexuality must be used in the context of love, of being shared with another person in love, or else it hurts God's feelings. This means that pornography and masturbation are not acceptable, because it is the taking of the deepest part of the human being and putting pleasure in it without love.

But, what about all the other things that the church condemns with regard to sexuality between two persons?

Let us see if we can figure this out.

If a man uses a prostitute, then while they are sharing the sexual act between each other (although it may also just be using her as a receptacle of his masturbation), this is obviously still being done for pleasure (or money) and not really out of a genuine love for the other person.

If two adults have consensual sex, but do not really love each other, and are just using each other for pleasure, then obviously it is the same problem.

The deepest part of the human being, the part that reflected the mystery upon which the universe is based, is being used for pleasure without love.

A husband feels hurt deeply when his wife goes with another man. God loves people more than a husband loves a wife, and He is even more sensitive than the husband is, because His love is more. When people seek lustful things without Him present, then He feels even more pain than the husband to the wife, because all sexuality was supposed to be shared with Him and He feels pain when it is not. He is the victim.

And how do you know that God is not present?

God is not present, because God is love and this has pleasure without love.

But what about if a boy and a girl have sex without marrying each other, but they love each other?

The answer to this is really simple: if they really do love each other, then that means they are going to spend the rest of their lives together. If they are unwilling to commit themselves like that, then obviously they do not really love each other. Love is not just a feeling; love is an action. If they really love each other, then, that means they would stay by each other when they felt happy and when they felt sad, when the feelings were there and when the feelings were gone.

If you only want to stay with the person as long as the

feeling lasts and then go find someone else once the feeling is gone, then this is not really love for the person, but rather it is love for the feeling. It is not real love, and hence if they have sex they are not really doing it with love for each other, because in fact they don't really love each, but they just love the feelings they have around each other.

If they really love each other, then they will be willing to make a commitment to stay together for the rest of their lives. And if they really are serious about this commitment, then of course they shouldn't feel anything wrong about setting it down in law and getting married, since in fact they really do plan to be with each other their whole lives. If they do not want to set it down in law for some reason other than this, but they still intend to seriously commit themselves for the rest of their lives as a certainty, then they can be counted as married. And if they can do that, then having sex becomes permissible, because it is being done in true love.

God is present then; He does not feel pain at being left out. The deepest part of the person, He is allowed to be with and is not being cut out of it. He is so very sensitive to them, but He is present in their sexual experience and so He feels no pain. He is present, because He is love.

But what about divorce?

Jesus did not say that those who divorce commit adultery, but rather He said that those who divorce and remarry commit adultery.

The truth is that this is really just the same as people who are not married but who go from one partner to another.

If a person plans to be with a person the rest of their lives in a loving relationship, only in this case can sexual activity be permissible. But if they really do plan to be with each other for their whole lives, then that means that they are not going to separate later and go marry someone else.

If they leave open the option that they may divorce and marry someone else later, then that only means that they are not really willing to set down with certainty that they will be with the person they are marrying the rest of their live.

If it was not morally permissible for a person before marriage to have sex, because they have not set down with certainty that they will be with their partner the rest of their lives, then it must also be true that leaving the door open to divorce and remarriage must be condemned as well for exactly the same reason. Since once you leave that door open, then that means you are not setting down with certainty you will be with the person the rest of your life.

1 Corinthians 13 says that ‘love endures all things’. If

you divorce and marry another, then your love for your spouse is not enduring all things, and thus it is not really love. It is impossible for marriage to have real love unless the door is closed to divorce. Because as long as you say you might leave and go for someone else, then your love is not true love, because it does not endure all things.

This door must be closed, or else the commitment to marriage is not really real.

The sin of divorce is not what the person does with the second partner, but it is the fact that they have sex with either partner without actually setting down a commitment that they will be with the person forever. If a person stays with the same partner their whole life, but they are never able to make a firm commitment that they will never leave, and the door is always open for divorce, then they never have real love. The door must be closed or else love is not real, because love endures all things.

And if the love is not real, then God is not there. If God is not there, then He feels suffering, like the husband does for his wife when she is with another man, because He loves us more than anyone and so He is sensitive to us more than anyone.

So, in order for this gift of sexuality to be shared with another person, it must be done with love, and if it is really love, then that means that they must be willing to set down a commitment to be with one another for the rest of their lives without leaving the possibility open of leaving each other to go after someone else.

This explains why sex outside of marriage and divorce is not permissible. It still doesn't explain the church's teaching regarding homosexual relations or contraceptives, however.

With regard to homosexual relations or with contraceptives, there is a common problem present in either one, which is that the sexual act is being completely removed from procreation and is not open to the gift of life.

He is really extremely sensitive to this, and the angels will try to make human beings understand with voiceless words that they are doing something against someone when they abuse sexuality like this.

When you enjoy any other thing in nature, it is not the same as this. You can eat food, drink beverages, sleep, have comfortable things, see beautiful sights, and tantalize your senses in many ways, and you don't need to share it with another person in love or else you commit sin.

This is because these things do not touch you as deeply as sexuality does. If a woman drinks tea without her husband and a woman has sex without her husband, the husband is more grieved about which one?

Sexuality was meant to be shared with God. We were created for Him. Every time sexuality is used without love, He feels more pain than the husband does for his wife, because God is so intimate and close to every human soul.

He is looking at His wife and seeing her committing adultery with the demons – this is His pain. Every time she masturbates, she is committing adultery with a demon. Every time she looks at pornography, she is committing adultery with a demon. Every time she has sex outside of marriage, she is committing adultery with a demon. Every time she has sex without love, she is having it with a demon and her husband is not present. If a man feels hurt when his wife goes to another man, then God feels even more hurt when human beings exclude Him from their sexuality and entertain demons instead, because we are His spouse.

When she does it with her spouse in a marriage open to life, she is doing it with God, because He is love and love is present. Even though they are doing it with each other, God is there with them. Similarly, the sacraments given in the Catholic Church, are actually given by Jesus, because it is Jesus in the priest who is hearing the confession, it is Jesus in the priest who is celebrating the

mass, it is Jesus in the priest who is baptizing someone
or preaching to someone.

But, if people do not know this, how can they be
blamed? It is because the angels will speak to people
with voiceless words throughout the world, both those
in the church and those outside of it. It doesn’t matter
whether it is in Italy, Brazil, Pakistan, China, Zambia…
the angels are everywhere, even where the faith is not,
and they will make people sense God’s displeasure
even if the people do not understand it. People and
societies will be made to sense that what they are doing
is wrong, even if they don’t have a clear reason why.

God wanted the deepest part of the person to always be
open in how it loved. This meant that when two people
had sex, not only did they need to have love for each
other, but they needed to also have love for others as
well.

In the gospel, Jesus says that whoever receives a child in
my name receives me, and whoever receives me
receives Him who sent me.

In this you come to understand that when a couple
opens themselves to the gift of receiving a child, then
they are opening themselves to Jesus by this and

thereby also opening themselves to the Father as well. When they are willing to have sex in a way that is open to the begetting of children, then the gift of sexuality is then no longer just being shared by these two, but it is also open to love of God and the love of someone who has not yet entered the world.

If people close the gift of sexuality to this, then they are closing this deepest part of themselves to anyone except themselves. 1 Corinthians 13 says that love 'does not seek its own', which means if the partners are doing this for themselves only, then it is not love.

Love does not seek its own, it is always open to others, or else it is not love. Hence, if the love between two people is closed to children, then it is also not truly love, because it is only for them and no one else.

When it is open to children, the love between the couples is then being opened to the world, because they are allowing new life to come into existence as a gift to this life, and the new life that may be produced can then give his love to the world. The love between the two then carries on through the child to be given to the world, and thus the love is no longer seeking its own, which means it is then true love where God is thus present.

And if it is not really love, then God is not present, and He feels hurt by that. In the Old Testament, it tells us that He slew Onan, the son of Judah, after Onan spilled his seed on the ground in order to avoid making Tamar pregnant, because the action angered God.

This refers to being open to children, but does not necessarily mean that children are in fact produced. If a couple is open to life, but no life comes because the pregnancy fails to be achieved, the love is still there because of the willingness to give to the world.

Even if people have never heard what the church said about contraceptives or they lived in a place or time where homosexual relations were acceptable or normal, it is still sinful, because the angels will speak to human beings with voiceless words that what they are doing is offensive, even if they do not understand how.

The truth is that a married heterosexual couple is not allowed to have sex in a way which is closed to procreation. If a married heterosexual couple cannot do this, then how is it 'homophobic' or 'hateful' to tell a homosexual couple that they cannot do it either? A man and a woman who are married are not permitted by God's law to have full oral or anal sex, or to have sexual relations in any way that it is impossible to procreate by, because this is closed to the gift of life. If it is impossible for them to do so, then obviously a gay couple cannot do so either.

Hence, even though it is right to discriminate between gay and straight couples, nevertheless it remains true that telling a gay couple they cannot have sex is not really discrimination at all- it is the same standard that is applied to heterosexual couples as well.

I am not really sure if my explanation as to why this victimizes God is really clear or not.

If God did not exist, then there would no reason why these things were sinful, because then there would be no victim. They would just be biological processes and people who are offended with it, would just be offended because they chose to be, and not because it hurt anyone. Without the victim there is no sin, but these things truly do have a victim.

If God did not love us and He did not care for us, such that He had no sensitivity towards what we did with our sexuality, then it would not be sinful because there is no victim. It is precisely because He is so close and intimate to human beings, that He is a God close to us and not far away from us, and therefore these things matter to Him and whether we share them with Him or not is the source of great pain or joy for Him.

If God was an energy force who had rules about how people should live in the universe and not a person with emotions or feelings, then all these rules governing sexuality would not make any sense. If God was not a person, there would be no victim.

Even the Soviet Union had taboos against sexual abuses and it jailed homosexuals. But if the human being was only biological (as the communists said) and there was no Creator to judge, then what was immoral about these things? And people know there is something wrong occurring and this knowledge itself points back to the Creator, and none of this knowledge would make sense if He were not a person.

It is because He is a person, with feelings, and He loves us and is so close to us, that sexuality bothers Him when it is not shared with Him. Like it or not, that is the way it is and the way it must be. The only alternative is for Him to just not be present, not to love us, not to be a Person who cares for us and is close to us... and would you prefer this?

I am not really sure if my explanation is making sense, so let me try one last attempt. Without a victim, there is no sin. God is a victim because we matter to Him. Possessing us, is like salvation to Him. Being deprived of us, to Him, is like the soul in hell being deprived of the sight of God.

Now, could you imagine if God loved the angels in heaven, enjoying perfect peace with them forever, and then just forgot about the human beings and let them stay on the Earth without coming to heaven? Could you imagine if the people who entered heaven were told that they would never be as happy as God was, because God decided He wouldn't share His joy with them, but only with Him and the angels?

If you think there is something wrong with this, then you understand how God feels when people share their sexualities with each other but close it to Him.

Imagine if He wasn't who He was, and He didn't in fact care about human beings. But He enjoyed perfect happiness in heaven while we were deprived of salvation forever. He lets us continue our lives on the Earth, but never lets us know who He is, never does anything for us, never helps us in any way and never shares His life with us. He is not sensitive to us at all; He doesn't care if we know Him or not.

If you think that there is something wrong with this, then you understand how God feels when people masturbate or watch pornography, or when people enjoy sexuality for pleasure without another person, because when they do that, the deepest part of themselves is being closed to Him.

A little child cries when the mother tells him she doesn't love him. God is even more sensitive to us than this child is to his mother.

God looks at human beings closing the deepest part of themselves to Him, is like if we see Him in heaven refusing to allow us to have paradise with Him.

So, if we think there is something wrong with this, then we know that treating God like this must not be right either. Because to Him, to be with us is heaven and to be deprived of us is hell. So, we must do to others as we would have others to do us, and since we would like to live in a world where God loves us as much as He does, then we must love Him in the same way and hold nothing back from Him.

So, these things bother God. Whether or not homosexuality bothers God more than all the other sexual sins that people commit and they are most atrocious of all sins. . . I am not so sure about this and actually I doubt it.

For example, I have difficulty understanding how a homosexual couple who commit their lives together could possibly be more offensive to God than a man who rapes female prostitutes, one after another, on a regular basis.

And yet, if you read the literature produced by many religious people on this subject, including even some quotations of the saints, they would have you believe that this gay couple is worse, because (they say) there is no other sin worse than homosexuality.

In 21ˢᵗ century Moscow, people who are black, people who are Chinese, Korean, or from any other non-Caucasian race who visit the city may find themselves targeted by skinheads and unemployed young people who harass or attack them with impunity. They have even killed people. The Russian Orthodox Church has spoken against this and the Russian government has taken some measures to fight it, but it remains rampant, not only in the capital, but in other regions as well. Russian society rejects homosexual relations, however, all sorts of other abuses of sexuality outside of a marriage open to procreation are widely found in Russian society.

If the angels who visited Lot were to go to Moscow today and they took on the appearance of two black men, perhaps they would get attacked on the streets, beaten badly and the police might do nothing to help them. Russia has the highest per capita abortion rate of any place in the world; far surpassing the western democracies... but it protects society from the gay culture.

If the same two angels walked around in San Francisco, Amsterdam, London, Toronto or New York, they would perhaps be left in peace. Even if they took up loudspeakers and said that sexuality was being abused through homosexuality and God was offended, but they didn＇t do it in a way that violated any law (carefully wording what they say to avoid violating hate crime laws as well), there is still a good chance they would be not be attacked, although some people might try to verbally abuse them and a few might even physically attack them. However, in such an event, the police might even come to protect them from other people who might try to attack them as they said these things.

Which of these places are really greater spiritual inheritors of Sodom?

If you think Sodom was just a question of homosexuality being present or not, then I suppose you would choose the latter, but if you think it was something deeper than that, then I am not sure it is as clear as that.

Ezekiel 16:49-50 Behold this was the iniquity of Sodom thy sister, pride, fulness of bread, and abundance, and the idleness of her, and of her daughters: and they did not put forth their hand to the needy, and to the poor. And they were lifted up, and committed abominations before me: and I took them away as thou hast seen.

The sin of Sodom, was this, but it had another dimension to it as well that can be found in the narrative.

Because in the Genesis narrative, Abraham spoke to God and God told Abraham that if there were just a few innocent people in Sodom, He would spare the whole place for their sake.

And when the angels came and visited Lot, the just person was not allowed to continue being just, because the people insisted that he let them have sex with these strangers, who were the angels in disguise. If the angels had come and visited Lot, and the people had left them in peace, the place would not have been destroyed.

Because as long as Lot was there, and he was allowed to continue being a just man without the society around him forcing him to follow the same sins that they did, then for his sake alone, the whole place would be spared. But once the society forced him to adopt the same sins that they did or face the consequences, then this place could no longer be spared, just as Abraham and God discussed.

The sin of Sodom is essentially this. As long as the just man remains in the place, then no matter how many sins the place has, the whole place is spared for the sake of the just few. But once the society no longer allows this just few to remain among them, then the whole place should be destroyed.

It is not really about homosexuality, homosexuality is just one example of how it could happen. If the society accepts homosexual sins and forces everyone else to sin with them, then this place if Sodom. But if the society accepts homosexual sins, but does not force the just few to sin with them, then this place is not Sodom.

It is for that reason that I say that no matter how much sexual degradation is occurring in the West, it still isn’t

Sodom, because there are still people who hold onto God and His law, and for their sake the whole place is thus spared, just as God promised to Abraham.

Like as Mary told in various apparitions, that people must pray and suffer for others in order for the world to avoid destruction.

The same is true of Moscow; even if we can list a whole array of sins that occur in that place, as long as there are still a just few living there and the society does not force them to sin with them, then the whole place is spared for their sake.

But there are places that do force the whole society to sin or else suffer death or imprisonment. Places like Nazi Germany, where refusal to hate Jews or engage in public acts against them could perhaps be met with serious consequences. And indeed, that state was destroyed very violently.

Or like in Stalin's Russia, where refusal to disavow God and raise your voice against innocents attacked by the party could merit consequences for yourself. And this was the country that Hitler invaded and gave great destruction to.

It doesn' t have to have any connection with homosexuality at all in order to be Sodom. There are many detestable things to God beyond just homosexuality.

In the bible, God speaking through the prophets compares Israel to Sodom. But this comparison says nothing about homosexuality. Instead when God speaks about Israel’s sins, it is more typically of idolatry in the context of a society that persecuted the people who spoke the Truth and rejected what was happening.

It is Sodom, because God spares the place for the sake of the just man, and the society no longer allows any just men to live among them.

If the whole society is taught to hate a particular group, and those who refuse to do so are attacked, whether this group is an ethnic minority, or even the church itself, then this society is Sodom. If the whole society requires people to tell lies or else they cannot work at their jobs and earn a living, then this place is Sodom. If the whole society requires people to worship an idol or suffer death, then this place is Sodom. If the whole society requires people to embrace sexual sins or be severely punished, then this place is Sodom.

Many of the western nations have been putting more and more pressure on its citizens to accept homosexuality, but we are still far from the point where a person who follows God’s law is not actually able to live there. There are people who are arrested and even imprisoned, but it is not because they are following God’s law, rather it is because they are breaking human law; they are able to follow God’s law and not break the human law, and the society will not arrest or imprison them; thus it is not Sodom, because the just man can still live there.

For example, the law might demand that an official has to sign on gay marriages or that nurses must assist in abortions, but there is no law that requires the person to actually work as the official or as the nurse. They can resign those positions and find other work, and continue to keep God's law in the same society.

At the very most, the law might require children to attend schools where they will be subject to indoctrination to get them to think a particular way that is opposed to God's law, however, if the children refuse to believe this indoctrination, there is no legal punishment for them.

It becomes harder to follow God's law in such a society, but it is not still Sodom, because the person who follows God's law is still capable of living within the society.

To live there with inconvenience perhaps, or to live there with various restrictions, but nevertheless he can live there and follow God's law, and the whole place is spared for his sake. People will be upset by this kind of unfairness and inconvenience, but it seems like a strange thing to be upset about – did not Christ say that whoever wants to be my disciple had to deny himself, take up his cross and follow me? If a person insists on always being treated fairly, he cannot be Christ's disciple.

There are two ways that this kind of situation can occur like as existed with Sodom, where the society no longer contained any just people living among them. One is by the whole society killing or destroying those who refuse to sin with them. The other is by the just few corrupting themselves and joining the sins of the rest. In either case, the end is the same, and God can no longer spare the place for the sake of the just few, because the just few are no longer there.

As far as the West is concerned, the latter seems like a bigger concern than the former, to my eyes. Because while the society does not really prevent people from following God's law, the amount of complicity in the sins of the society by even those who think they follow God is really quite great. But as long as there are some people out there doing what Mary asked at Fatima, and continuing in their prayer, and not falling into sin, the whole place will be spared from destruction for their sake.

So, the sin of Sodom is not necessarily homosexuality at all. It can be this, but it does not need to be, it can be many other things as well.

But that still doesn't answer the question as to whether homosexuality is really more terrible than all other sins.

I believe that homosexual acts bother the Lord very much, but I don＇t believe it is possible that He holds homosexuals in a greater guilt than many heterosexuals who abuse their sexuality, simply because they are homosexual.

There are many homosexuals who abuse their sexuality to an astounding degree, going through so many partners that they just use for sex and not for love, indulging in all sorts of other vices along the way. But if you were to condemn these people as great sinners, it was more so because of their extreme behaviour than it is was the fact that they did it with men rather than with women.

In the gospel, the Lord condemns various cities and claims that if the signs done in them had been done in Sodom or Gomorrah, then those cities would have repented long ago, but in the judgment Sodom will be punished less than these places. Evidently therefore, the sin of Sodom was not the greatest of all sins.

The sin of these places was greater was because they had been shown more and yet they still didn＇t repent. What made the sin greater or lesser evidently was based on how much God had given to them.

Consider for a moment the person with homosexual preferences in the modern-day. Suppose that this person has sexual feelings almost entirely for their own sex and not for the opposite sex. Now this is a big temptation for them. However, unlike the heterosexual, they have no way of escaping this temptation by just marrying the opposite sex and ending the burning of their lust. It is therefore *harder* for them to conquer these lusts, than it would be for a person who was able to get married in a legitimate relationship.

Now if the heterosexual still abuses sexuality, even though he can find a way to cure such lusts through marriage, and the homosexual abuses sexuality... is it not the heterosexual who has the greater guilt? Seeing that more had been given to him, and yet he still did not change?

Christ said that Sodom's sin was less than the sin of those places He preached to, because Sodom had less opportunity to repent than these places, and yet these places still did not repent.

In the early church, when the Roman authorities demanded Christians to reject Jesus and worship the Emperor under penalty of death, many Christians gave in and worshipped the emperor. And when they tried to come back to the church later they were often refused to come back, or perhaps only allowed to come back after very extreme penance was undertaken, because their sin in abandoning Christ was seen as so great.

Now, in the modern day, vast numbers of Catholics leave the church and do not come back again. Not because there is a gun pointed at their heads, but just because they don’t want to go anymore for one reason or another. And Catholics may even try to reach out to them, calling on them to ‘come home’, not demanding massive penance from them.

In reality, which of these two groups had the greater sin? The Catholics in the early church needed a sword over their heads to leave the faith, and only for a brief moment, but the Catholics of the modern day needed no such thing at all to convince them to abandon the faith for many years. How can it not be that the latter had a greater sin than the former? But the church demanded extreme penance from the former and perhaps did not even forgive them at all at that time, but in our time, they give them welcome and may treat them like they did nothing wrong at all.

I don’t believe that God looks at human sins the same way that human beings do. I think He applies standards with justice and fairness, and in Truth and Love. If most people think that morality is different from how He sees things, it does not matter, He remains the same.

Lord, your law is a delight to us and we thank you for revealing it to us. Please help us to understand your law and follow it in our lives. We pray for mercy upon all those who don＇t, and we pray that you make us instruments to bring people back to following your laws. We ask for these things, if it is your will, in Jesus＇ name, Amen

III: Sexual Complementarity

All sexual acts that are either removed from love in a permanent relationship or are removed from love through procreation are not permissible.

However, there is another dimension to this that needs to be said. Because homosexual acts are not against the moral law for this reason alone. If somehow, sometime in the future, a new technology was created that somehow allowed for a same-sex couple to have sex in a way that made one of them pregnant, and thus the act was open to life, it still would not be allowed.

This is because there is also an issue of sexual

complementarity involved as well.

Men were designed for sexual relationship with women, and vice-versa. Their psychologies and personalities are designed like this.

It is possible for men to love men emotionally and for women to love women emotionally. It is perhaps even possible for men to live their lives with men and women to live their lives with women, and for them to be happy together.

However, it is not possible for them to love each other in a sexual relationship and be happy like this, because they are not designed like this.

There are gay people, who try to find qualities of the opposite sex within a partner of the same sex, because they can' t really feel happy about being sexually intimate with a same-sex partner who really does resemble a normal man or woman.

This is touching upon the sexual complementarity I am speaking about.

Even though they have sexual feelings for the same sex, the men may still possess the brains of men and the women may still possess the brains of women, and genetically they may be programmed to be happier with qualities in a sexual partner that resemble the opposite sex rather than the same-sex. Even though they have a same-sex attraction, this simply cannot be undone. Even if they live together for years, it will still follow them and the sexual relationship will not be able to flourish because of it.

Even if somehow it were possible for them to procreate and they devoted themselves to each other for the rest of their lives, they would still find that something was wrong because of this fact.

It is perhaps a bit like saying that even if people are sincerely seeking for the Truth in another religion, they still cannot know God intimately until they come to be baptized and receive the Eucharist. No matter what another religion offers, no matter how good it is, no will ever be able to come to God and be with Him intimately until they do this. Because the other religion is a created thing like them, and they were designed for the Creator.

If there exist gay couples who can live together in a sexual relationship and be totally happy with one another, then what I have written above could not be true- at least not for them, although perhaps for others.

It would mean that somehow, they did have sexual complementarity, even though they are a same-sex couple.

If they were indeed like this, and they had sexual

complementarity, then they still would not be morally allowed to have sex, however, for the same reasons that heterosexual couples cannot have sex without procreation.

If in the future some way was created whereby they could have sex with procreation, then I think there are no more arguments why we should find anything wrong about it, seeing that they have sexual complementarity.

Now, does this exist?

There are countless examples in existence of homosexual relationships which were never able to truly have the intimate relationship of two spouses, and no matter what semblances were placed around it, they were never able to have what a man and a woman had in marriage.

However, to simply say this does nothing at answering the question as to whether this exists or not. If 99% of gay relationships cannot function properly because they are gay relationships, but 1% can even though they are gay relationships, then the answer to the question is then an affirmative, that yes, the sexual complementarity can exist.

But, it shouldn't exist. Not even with 1% - not even with a single couple, anytime, anywhere. Otherwise what the church is saying is wrong.

At least according to how we understand the church's deposit of teachings regarding the human being, it should not exist. It should not be possible for two men or two women to live in a sexual relationship and be truly happy in it. If it is possible, then that means they have sexual complementarity, which doesn't make any sense if God created the human being to be exclusively heterosexual.

There are theologians in the church today who want to disregard the church's doctrines in favour of looking at the lived experiences of people. In principle, I don't think they are wrong.

Because, if you investigate the lives of people, you ought to find the proof of the church's doctrines within their lives. There is no greater proof to show that the Catholic Church is right in its moral teachings than the actual lived evidence of people who follow these teachings or not.

And really, there are thousands of cases out there of homosexual relationships that are so deeply flawed that the church's teachings about the person are being proved by them.

Now, what happens if you actually find that people are in a relationship that the church's teachings considers objectively disordered, and yet they are completely happy?

If they really are happy, and it is not just a semblance or a suppression of their true unhappiness; if they are not just pretending to be happy and living in a lie they construct around them; if they truly are like this, and you can truly confirm it as so, then you have to accept their experiences over our understanding of the church＇s teachings.

The church＇s teachings are confirmed by reality, if they are not confirmed by reality, then it is not reality that has the problem, it is the teachings that have the problem or rather it is our understanding of the church＇s teachings that have the problem.

Because truth cannot contradict truth. The church teachings cannot be false, and yet reality cannot be false either.

If reality is like this, then somehow, we must have misunderstood what the church taught, if the teachings are not actually borne up by reality. We do not reject reality in favour of the teachings, but rather we look to reality as the proof that the teachings are true.

We cannot say to them, ＇you shouldn＇t be happy with each other, you ought to be miserable with each other, it is not possible that you are truly happy with each other, so please reject what you see and experience and believe what we tell you＇.

It is not possible that you can say that they are

disordered, because if they were, then they ought to be unhappy in the relationship. They have sexual complementarity... but they shouldn't.

There are gay people who live in relationships with each other for 20, 30, 40 years··· even their whole lives until death. And they seem to be happy in the relationships as well, although truth be told, even long years can disguise miserableness in a relationship.

But, I am hesitant to say if they really are all, every last one of them, ultimately miserable in these relationships, which is exactly what the church doctrine would require to be true or else the doctrine was seemingly false.

Let us suppose that they are not miserable··· how could this be explained within what the church knows about the human being?

Sexual complementarity between members of the same sex is still impossible and it does not exist.

But suppose, it is possible that these couples are focused more on the emotional side than the sexual side of the relationship, and while it is impossible for a homosexual couple to have sexual complementarity, perhaps it is possible that they may have some deep level of emotional complementarity and the relationship can flourish on this basis. It is possible they don't have sex very often and doesn't form an important part of the relationship. They like each other for their personalities, but not really for sex.

The church's teachings do not forbid that from existing. We are not made sexually for one another, but maybe the emotional side of a relationship is something that can happen between the same-sex and yet be happy and not miserable, even over a long period of time.

However, suppose indeed there are homosexual relationships in which sex is an important component and they last for decades, while the members within the relationship are satisfied and essentially happy⋯at least as happy as a married couple who had sex but failed to have children⋯ this would seem to strike a blow to what the church teaches about the nature of men and women.

It is a reality that appears totally inconsistent with what the church teaches about the human being.

However, the church cannot be wrong, and true sexual complementarity between members of the same sex is still impossible and it does not exist.

Despite the happiness seemingly present, we can still be suspicious about this and second-guess whether they really are as happy as they seem. It may be the case that there is no sexual union anywhere between members of the same sex, which is not miserable over time, and it just appears otherwise because it is disguised to us.

But if it really does exist⋯

If so, then there must be another explanation for it, in which the church's teaching remains true. I have a guess at what the answer may be, and I will talk about this more later when we get to the topic of 'born gay'.

Lord, we pray that you help us to live our lives according to the nature of the gender you gave to us and help remove all forms of discomfort associated with it. We pray that you help all people to accept the gift of their masculinity and femininity with joy. We ask for these things, if it is your will, in Jesus' name, Amen

Part II: LGBT Issues

In the second part of this book, I am going to go over a number of specific LGBT issues.

The reason why homosexual acts are not permissible within Catholic teaching is all found in the above section. However, there are still a number of specific issues I want to go through one by one.

IV: Crossdressing

In itself there is nothing either right or wrong about wearing a piece of clothing. However, what people feel when wearing it, what other people feel when seeing it, and what the motivations behind wearing it were, can determine whether it was right or not.

With regard to crossdressing there are mainly two places where a sin may be present. The first is that if the person wears clothing of the opposite sex because there is some sexual feeling related to the wearing of the article of clothing. This may be more common for men dressing in women's clothes than the other way around. It is not an uncommon thing, and it is not at all a shameful thing that a person should have such feelings either.

If the man experiences a sexual feeling from wearing women's clothing, and he does it on his own, then it is just another form of masturbation, and is therefore a perversion of sexuality by taking his innermost self and filling it with pleasure without love.

However, if with his wife in the sexual act that is open to life, he was to wear such clothes then it is not a bad thing at all; rather it is a good thing, so long as his wife is not uncomfortable with it.

The second place where sin may be present, is that cross-dressing is likely to provoke discomfort and scandal among many people, in almost every culture in the world. However, not necessarily among all people at all times everywhere.

Hence, because creating scandal and offending people, except when it is of necessity to do so, is sinful, therefore cross-dressing must also be sinful if it does this.

Even if the person who wears the clothes does not want to hurt anyone's feelings, if he knows that people are going to be offended and scandalized by it, then unless there is some very important reason why he needs to cross-dress, then he must not do so.

Paul said that we should try to seek to please people in all things. He tried to become all things to all men. Only if it was necessary, would he say something that was offensive to people, and that necessity was the salvation of their souls.

In the same way, we have to avoid doing things that upset people's sensibilities, whether it is this subject or any subject. If wearing a particular kind of clothing or doing a particular type of activity is going to anger or scandalize people in a particular place, then you shouldn't do so unless there is an important reason why you need to do so.

If eating with your fingers at table offends people, then you don't eat with your fingers at table, unless it is necessary to do so. If spitting on the flag of the country offends people, then you don't spit on the flag of the country, unless it is necessary to do so. If smoking or chewing gum offends people, then you don't smoke or chew gum, unless it is necessary to do so. If calling people after a certain hour at night is going to annoy them, then you can call them at another time, unless there is some necessity. If singing in public annoys people, then you can stop singing in public to make them happy. If not wearing deodorant upsets people, then you can wear it to please them.

Cross-dressing is not a special activity in this regard; anything that is unnecessary, which is likely to cause offence and scandal to people, is sinful if done. Because you are hurting people's feelings without a due reason for why they need to be hurt, so you do not do so.

It is so amazing to watch the modern western society, and see how it is offended by people who hand out new testaments in front of synagogues, or how it is offended by people who preach about Jesus on the street, and by doing so they then bear witness that they themselves know it to be wrong to offend the feelings of people. And yet preaching the gospel is the most necessary of all things. If it is wrong to offend people, then obviously public cross-dressing, and in fact any public display of sexuality that offends people must be wrong.

However, if cross-dressing is done in such a circumstance in which people are not offended- like among a group of friends or in some place, some time in history, when it is sociable and acceptable- and furthermore the cross-dressing is asexual in nature, then there is nothing wrong with it.

For example, in theatre shows of past times when boys dressed in the part of women, it was not necessarily an evil to do so, because it was neither scandalous nor sexual.

Whether it is psychologically helpful or harmful for the person⋯ is an entirely different topic⋯ because there are things that may be psychologically harmful, but the person engaging in them may not be committing a sin against God by doing so, because he may sincerely think he is not doing any such harm.

If he knows it is psychologically harmful (whether it is or not- I am not the expert) and he does it, then yes, it is a sin in the same way that any other self-harm is.

In the bible, it says that it is an abomination for people to cross-dress. It was for this reason that Joan of Arc was burned at the stake, because she wore man's clothes and said that God was her guide, and so the Inquisition said she was following the devil. She did not cross-dress out of sexual desire, but rather she did so out of necessity. It was true that her crossdressing did provoke scandal, but in her case, it was necessary, since contemporary women's clothing could not be practically used by someone engaging in combat or fulfilling the mission she was given, and it was God's commandment to her to take up arms.

It is not wrong in itself to wear clothing of the opposite sex; it is just a question of whether it be sexual or asexual, scandalous or not scandalous. If it is sexual, but it is done with a spouse and open to life, then of course it is not sinful and in fact it is good thing.

Lord, we pray that you help human beings to use cross-dressing in a way that is not scandalous or in violation of your moral law. We pray that people who have the desire to cross-dress will have this desire fulfilled licitly and not illicitly within your law. We ask for these things, if it is your will, in Jesus' name, Amen

V: Emotional Same-Sex attraction

There is no one who is created as gay. The marriage in

heaven between the Bride and Bridegroom is reflected upon the Earth by our natures, whether feminine or masculine.

Men are designed to marry women, and women are designed to marry men. We are like this, because we are a reflection of that divine union.

If people can find salvation through created things or Christ can be contented by living with the Trinity and not going to save human beings, then that is like saying that the Bride can marry the Bride and the Bridegroom can marry the Bridegroom. If salvation outside the church is possible, then gay marriage is possible too.

God is not a reflection of us, we are rather a reflection of Him. We were created as men and women to reflect the nature of this marriage; this marriage was not created as a reflection of what we do.

But if this marriage is not like this, and people do not need to be united with the Creator for salvation, and the Trinity can be content with each other and without saving us, then surely men can also marry men and women can marry women, because these two mysteries are speaking of the same thing.

The entire reason why our genders and our sexualities are like this is because of the fact we are made in God's image and are reflections of the marriage in heaven. If this marriage in heaven is not like this, then marriage on Earth is not like this either.

If the original is not this way, then how could the copy
be this way?

It is a greater mistake to say that salvation is possible
without the church than it is to say that same-sex
marriage is possible, because the latter is the abuse of a
copy and the former is an abuse of the original. It is a
greater example of bad witness when we tell people
they do not need the church to get to heaven, than it is
to tell people that homosexual relationships are OK,
because the latter is the copy and the former is the
original.

If you, a created thing, can find salvation through
another created thing and not through the Creator, and
the Trinity can be eternally content with themselves
only, then why would the sexes, which were created as a
copy of this mystery, need to be otherwise?

The entire mystery of human sexuality is founded in the
marriage in heaven; if that marriage is not heterosexual
and the human being can be satisfied with the religions
he creates himself without the Truth that comes from
God or that God never actually sent a Messiah to save
human beings, then how could we possibly fault
someone for claiming that homosexuality is natural,
seeing that we are already claiming that the marriage in
heaven can be homosexual?

I don’t think it is any accident that the gay liberation

movement globally came from the same period in which the church opened up to other religions after Vatican II. Because so many Catholics came to think that people outside the church were saved as well while following other religions, thus there was no longer any need to convert them, even though the church has explicitly taught the opposite in the past, and yet if they were saved while following created religions, then the bride can marry the bride and the bridegroom can marry the bridegroom.

God uses persecution and trial to clean the church of its errors and sins as a goldsmith uses fire to cleanse gold of its impurities. Augustine taught that the challenge of heresies made the church's teachings stronger in the end. I suspect that God is using the gay liberation movement as a hammer to discipline His church for all of the errors that have come from this issue. In the end the church will be stronger because of it, and understand its own teaching better than it did before.

When the church is challenged by the gay culture, people are forced to contemplate, why exactly it was that the church teaches that God does not make people gay. And in finding the answer, they will be forced to understand their own faith more deeply about the nature of the marriage in heaven.

The church's teachings cannot be changed. Same-sex marriage shall never be possible, and salvation shall never exist outside of the church.

People in other religions could only possibly get to heaven through the church, and not through other religions. If all they know about the church is just the Truth presented by God, spread by His angels with voiceless words, within the culture they live in, then they can follow this and get to heaven; but this Truth they follow is still part of the Catholic faith and therefore there is still no one outside the church who can find salvation.

Now, within the church, however, we honour many saints and angels. We do so many things for them: we have statues of them, we burn candles in front of their images, we make prayers to them, we have celebrations of them, their names are included in the mass, we name people after them, and we give them all sorts of respects and devotions.

In a certain way, we often treat these saints and angels the way that polytheistic religions treated their myriads of gods, with each god representing a different portfolio he was responsible for and able to help people in different ways.

These people are not the Trinity, however, and salvation does not come from them. They are One with God in heaven, and thus they can also be said to have become one flesh with God, in the way that the wife becomes one flesh with her husband, but we cannot find our salvation from them.

However, we place upon them so many honours and devotions, which may seem like we are treating them as God, even though we do not consider them God.

We are not worshipping them, however. Our worship to God is done in the mass, and the mass is offered up to the Father. The mass cannot be offered up to Mary or a saint.

Similar to a marriage, you can have your spouse and love him or her exclusively, but that doesn't mean you can't also have many other people in your life who are close to you and who you are friends with. Sex, however, can only be done with your spouse, not with your friends. In just the same way, we can honour people who are not God, but worship God alone.

Now, how close is it possible to deeply love and live with another person you are not married with, without committing a sin?

If people who are not married live together their whole lives and they in fact love each other emotionally and deeply, almost like they were soul mates, but they do not have sex, and their proximity to each other is not a temptation to have sex, then church teaching would not condemn this. If they slept in the same bed and hugged each other each night, but there was no sexual experience or temptation between them, the church teaching would not condemn this.

It is similar to saying that you honour a saint so much, that you pray to the saint, have pictures of the saint in your house, name your child after the saint, ask the saint to help bring you to salvation, almost as though you treat the saint like God, while still going to mass and knowing that salvation comes from God and the saint is just interceding for you to help you get it.

It is like you are treating the saint as God, but you are not really doing so, and you are not falling into idolatry.

However, this devotion is not found in the bible. Michael and other angels get honoured in the Old Testament (human beings did not yet go to heaven, so we can't talk about saints in that time before Jesus' resurrection), but the Israelites did not have the sort of practices that we do today of praying to them, burning candles in front of statues of them, having religious devotions to them or anything like this. And God never told them to do so, either.

And I think that He could not have asked them to do so, because the Israelites were always a very stubborn people who often abandoned God in order to worship idols. Hence, if God revealed at that time that having such a devotion to an angel in heaven like Michael was actually a good thing, the Israelites would then find it much easier to embrace their idolatry and go after other gods. So, to stop an evil from happening, you must ban something that is good because this is necessary to end the evil. The Israelites were not even allowed to erect pillars, because the nations around them worshipped pillars.

It would be OK for people to live their lives together and love each other so long as the sexual aspect was removed, in the same way that it is OK for people to honour saints and angels as though they were God without actually worshipping them. Like Mary and Joseph, a couple that loved each other as a couple and had no sexual contact.

However, because the temptation to sin is likely to remain, and very few people are able to live together like Mary and Joseph without committing sin, therefore this probably is still not advisable for most people in the world who do have a desire for a same-sex relationship. It is better to be lonely all one's life than it is to commit sin even once.

It is possible for a person who is married to have a friend outside of marriage who is like a soul mate, and yet not have a sexual relationship with this person. And if the husband is very generous, he will not only tolerate it, but he will happy for his wife. So is Christ to the church, when the church honours the saints.

But, I am speaking here not just of same-sex couples,

but of anyone at all who loved another person in a non-sexual relationship.

David loved Jonathan as he loved his own soul, and said that his love was greater than the love of women, although David was heterosexual and had many wives; he even committed adultery with the wife of another man.

But, Jonathan was not a spouse to David.

It is like this, I think: any kind of emotional love that people have for each other is not banned by the church teaching.

If two people of the same sex really are happy living like a couple with each other and without sex, then there is nothing in the church teaching that condemns this.

But, whether this actually exists or not is a different question. It may be the case that such people do not exist, and those who do live together for long periods are not really happy together, because God did not design for people of the same sex to live with one another like this.

I suspect that there are people who were designed to

have deep emotional relationships with other people of the same sex, perhaps even emotionally deeper than they do with the opposite sex, but as sisters and brothers, not as spouses. Like David and Jonathan.

But then again, perhaps there are, I don't know. Again, one has to point to the gay couples who live together for decades and ask how it is possible that it stands like this for so long, if it was not the case that they had a genuine emotional love for each other?

If there are people who feel that they want to have an emotional relationship with someone of the same sex and the possibility of the relationship becoming sexual is not a serious risk, there is nothing that the church can say that they are not allowed to do this.

Whether it exists or not, I don't know, but there is nothing in the church teaching that condemns it so long as the sexual aspect is completely removed.

Lord, we pray that you give us wisdom concerning these things. We pray that whatever your plan is regarding these things, you will help us to discern it and to follow it. We ask for this, if it is your will, in Jesus' name, Amen

VI: Born Gay?

One of the biggest debates around this topic surrounds the issue as to whether people are born gay or not.

On the one hand, you have a large number of people, often affiliated with religions, who maintain that no one is created as gay and rather it is something that occurs in the person's psychological development that causes them to develop these attractions.

On the other hand, you have another group of people, who may be religious or not, who insist that people are born with the homosexual orientation and it cannot be changed.

On either side of this debate you also have a number of people themselves who have struggled with or embraced homosexual attractions, voicing their own personal experiences insisting that they were born this way and they cannot be changed, or that they had such an attraction and they got over it or recognize that this was not the way that God made them.

There are also psychologists and neural scientists who deal with the brain and human psychology, who stand on either side of this debate, asserting the presence of evidence in favour of either suggestion.

I am neither a psychologist nor a neural scientist, and while I have read some of the literature produced on the subject, I am afraid I must leave most of that scientific debate to other people more qualified than myself to speak on these things.

In the Catechism it says 'its psychological genesis is unknown'.

This therefore means that the church takes no official position on what the exact cause to homosexuality is.

The church has the authority to tell people that God created the world, but it does not have the authority to tell people how the creation happened in terms of science. Similarly, the church has the authority to tell people that homosexuality is a disordered condition, but it has no authority to state what scientific factors cause it.

That being said, there are many Catholics who believe that they do know what causes it.

There are organizations within the church which are designed to help people with same sex desires and which teach them that homosexual desires arise from a psychological condition and they may even speak about the alleged psychological causes in their official literature, preaching or presentations. For example, they may teach that men have homosexual desires because they had trouble accepting masculine role models as a child and so they adopted feminine ones, and then found the same sex to be attractive because it was like the opposite sex to them.

I feel that what these Catholic organizations are doing, is actually something dangerous, although they are not doing it with bad intent.

There is nothing wrong with speaking about these possible theories of what causes homosexual attractions…as theories. As a scientific debate among people looking for understanding, it is absolutely fine.

The problem enters in when these theories are put in the official literature or preaching of organizations like these with church approval, which in fact carries the church's teaching authority, then it tends to make people who come to these organizations for help to think like these theories *are* the church's official position and not just the private opinions of the members who run these organizations.

And the church's official position is exactly what it says in the catechism 'its psychological genesis is unknown'. Hence, when they put down these theories as fact, they are inadvertently saying that the catechism is wrong and that the psychological genesis is known.

The church takes no position on the scientific causes of things. It teaches truths about God and about the human person, but the specific scientific things are not within the church's authority to speak on.

If a cleric teaches something scientific, but the scientific fact is one that is not questioned, then it is not so dangerous. If a priest says, for instance, that gravity is caused by masses that pull each other together, and he is not speaking about this as though it were a doctrine from the church that needed to be accepted, but simply as a fact that science considered true, which he was using to make some comment upon in his religious teaching, there is not much risk here of deceiving or hurting people.

I say it is dangerous what these organizations are doing on this point, because if in fact the theories they are teaching are found to be false or inaccurate, then they damage the credibility of the church. They also bind the consciences of people by making them think that they are going against church teaching if they entertain other scientific theories, when in fact the church never took a position on scientific facts to begin with.

I think that if they want to teach these theories to the people who come to them for help, then they must make it clear that these are just their own beliefs and not the official church position. No Catholic is obligated to accept them.

The reason why they may want to teach these theories is a good one, however. Because many people will claim that God made people gay and therefore how can He blame them if they have sex? If they were made by God like this, then how can it be unnatural to have a homosexual relationship?

Therefore, in order to stop people from thinking like this and to save their souls, these organizations may try to emphasize that no one is born gay, that the reason why a person develops these feelings is not from nature and therefore they can't say that it was God's desire for them to do these things.

In other words, these organizations are saying these things in order to stop people from sinning and going to hell. It is not a bad motivation.

The problem is, if in fact these theories are false, then rather than helping people to change, they may end up distancing people from the church and leading people to think that the church's voice cannot be trusted.

Furthermore, if the theories are false and people are in fact born gay, they could be actually opposing God by teaching like this. They are telling people to then reject themselves. I will talk about this more later.

Therefore, whatever good intentions they had, I don't think it is right to teach these theories in such an official capacity, unless it is accompanied by a clear indicator that they are theories only and not the official position of the church. People can say that in their own opinions that such theories are true, but it is very dangerous once you put the church's name on it and teach it in an official capacity as an organ of the church as some of these organizations have done.

The truth is that you don't need to prove the causes of homosexuality in order to judge homosexual actions as wrong. As I wrote above, if even a married heterosexual couple cannot have sex in a way that children cannot be produced, then you know that no matter what is said about the causes of homosexuality, nothing can possibly change about the fact that homosexual acts cannot be accepted by the church.

Even if God made them this way, even then nothing can change about the fact that they cannot have sex in catholic teaching.

The human brain is not well enough understood in our own time for people to really answer the question of how the structures in the brain cause or affect human sexuality.

However, the idea itself that the brain could be designed to recognize differences in sexes and to be designed to have sexual attractions to one sex or another, is not an outlandish idea.

There are robots that are designed today that are able

to look at a person's face and determine if the person was male or female, and they are programmed to give different responses to the person on the basis of the gender that the robot perceives.

The human brain is just a computer. Human beings are biological robots that have conscious souls inhabiting them. A person feels sad when skies are grey and feels happy when it is sunny, because the brain is programmed to make them feel this way. A person desires to eat fatty foods and does not have such a great craving for vegetables, because the brain is programmed to make them feel this way. A person feels angry when he perceives he is treated unfairly by others and he feels happy when he feels respected by others, because the brain itself is programmed like this.

Similarly, the boy finds the girl to be sexually attractive or the girl finds the boy to be sexually attractive, because the brain is programmed like this. They are just robots with programming that is set into their neurons that fire electric signals and make the person feel and experience everything the person feels and experiences. But what makes the human being different from a robot, is that the robot has no soul, no consciousness, and cannot choose to follow its programming or not – it just does. The human being, however, has a soul, a consciousness, and can choose to follow its programming or not.

A question being debated is whether or not it is possible

that a human brain is arranged in such a way that it is designed to see the same sex as sexually attractive rather than the opposite sex. Like the robot that recognizes the face and can make a different response on the basis of the sex, so also the human brain sees a member of the same sex, and its biological programming leads it to feel lust.

This book, however, cannot answer that – what it can answer, however, is how such things relate to doctrine.

Now, as I said the church cannot answer specific scientific questions but there are truths about the human person that it does uphold. I am going to go through several hypotheses about what causes homosexuality and discuss whether they are acceptable or not within Catholic doctrine concerning the truths about the human person.

1) Psychology

A psychological explanation for homosexuality has no contradiction with Catholic doctrine.

The Catechism in fact implicitly assumes that the explanation for homosexuality is psychological, because it says 'its psychological genesis is unknown'. There is an important reason why it assumes this, which I will discuss in the second option on biology.

This explanation is the simplest and easiest explanation. All people are created as heterosexual, and biologically they are designed as heterosexual. But somehow, as a result of what happens after birth, in the environment they are raised in and the development of their mind, they develop homosexual attractions. However, their biology and sexualities remain heterosexual in nature, but they have just been warped against their true nature by environment or other non-biological factors.

They are ultimately heterosexual in nature, but they just psychologically develop a same-sex attraction as an aberration of their true nature and not as something that actually belongs to the way their brains or bodies were designed to work.

This has no contradiction at all with Catholic doctrine.

It is a bit like saying that all people are designed for God, but because of the effects of original sin, they instead seek after created things and created religions instead.

2) Biological

By biological, I mean that the person is in fact born with a biology that is in fact designed to be sexually attracted by the same sex. This is different from the psychological origin, because the psychological origin (as I define it) means that the person has a brain and sexuality designed for the opposite sex, and it simply develops psychologically to have a sexual attraction for the same sex, whereas the biological origin (as I define it) implies that the brain and biology itself is designed to be attracted to the same sex. That is to say it is not because of environment or other external factors, but because of nature itself that the person developed this attraction.

Can a biological explanation be reconciled with Catholic doctrine?

Firstly, it must be acknowledged that church teaching states that God does not create people as gay; it is impossible in Catholic teaching.

We are made as reflections of the marriage in heaven; a woman by her femininity reflects the bride, and the man in his masculinity reflects the bridegroom. And because both the bride and the bridegroom become one flesh and thus become God together, therefore both natures are reflections of the divine.

If a man was designed for a man or a woman for a woman, then they no longer reflect this. Hence, this cannot be undone. No one can possibly be created gay.

The entire fabric of all reality, from the beginning of the universe to its end, from the first day of creation to the second coming··· nothing exists without a reference to this mystery of the marriage in heaven. It absolutely cannot be undone.

If homosexuality is from biological causes, does that mean it is the way that God created the person?

This is an important question to consider.

Now, there are many ways that people are born with deformities. There are people that are born without eyes, people who are born blind, people who are born without hearing, people born without limbs, people who have heart defects from birth, people who are missing parts of their brain when they are born, people who are in a vegetative state from their birth··· and so on..

When they go to heaven, when they are resurrected from the dead, it is often assumed that they will not need to have these deformities anymore.

All these things are biological; they are born like this.

There are people who have brain injuries after they are born and who lose some function that they had before as a result of the injury. This is a biological change, and it is not the way that God created the person. If a scientist performs a lobotomy on an adult, it is the scientist who changed the brain, not God, but it is biological.

That being said, however, there is something in this that needs to be noted. When Jesus resurrected from the dead, He did so with His wounds still on His body. It was human beings who gave Him these wounds and not God, but His resurrected body had the wounds on it.

What I say in the following part, I say this on my own as a speculation, in considering the truths of Jesus' resurrection, about what I think must be true for all of us: in the resurrection, both the deformity and the condition of body without the deformity, in a mysterious way, will both belong to the person resurrected.

In a person's life, their bodies change throughout their lives. They go from being babies, to being children, to being adults and to being old persons. When the person is resurrected, all of these stages in life will belong to the resurrected person, in a mysterious way. There is nothing that a person had when they were a child, with a child's body and a child's personality that they will not also have once again in the resurrection. There is nothing that a person had when they were elderly, with an elderly person's body and an elderly person's personality, which they will not also have once again in the resurrection.

They will have every stage of life in the resurrection given back to them, along with the scars and injuries as well as the state of the body without the scars and injuries, but all of these things will be in such a way that no one will feel any kind of suffering over it.

What this will look like, and how it is possible for a person to have all stages of their life given back to them, I do not know and I cannot explain. But in short, there is nothing that the person has in life which will not also belong to them in the resurrection, but in a perfect and glorious way.

The wounds of Jesus belong to Him forever, as do the wounds of the martyrs, as do the wounds of all people at all times. But the state of the body without the wound will also belong to the person at the same time. The changes that occur in the physical body in life will all belong to people In the resurrected state, and the state of the body without the changes will also belong to people in the resurrected state as well.

The man born blind will have both blindness and vision in the resurrection. The person born in the vegetative state will possess both the vegetative state and the animated state in the resurrection. Nothing they had in life will be taken from people, but they will have it and have even more in the resurrection.

I think we can know this by looking at Jesus Himself. How many times has He appeared in apparitions down the ages as the infant Jesus, the child Jesus, the adult Jesus, the crucified Jesus, the resurrected Jesus, the Jesus with the wounds, the Jesus without the wounds and so on? He has all these things in heaven that He had in life; every stage in life He went through will belong to Him forever. If this is so with him, then I think it must also be so with the rest of humanity.

The deficiencies people had in life in fact will be glorified in the resurrection. The person born blind will have both vision and blindness, but his vision perhaps will be greater than those who had vision in life. The person born in a vegetative state will have both this and the animated state, but perhaps in an even greater way than those who were not in a vegetative state in life. The person who had his hands cut off for Christ will have both the handless state and the state with the hands in the resurrection, but his hands will perhaps be something greater than it was for those who did not lose their hands in life.

Just as in the gospel Jesus promised that whatever they gave up for God, God will give them back even more.

I cannot say this certainty, as it is my speculation and it

is neither church doctrine or revealed prophecy, but I suspect it is like this.

When Jesus met the man born blind, they asked him 'who sinned, was it this man or his parents, which made him born blind?' And Jesus said that neither he nor his parents sinned, but his blindness was for the glory of God.

I interpret this as meaning not only his parents, but even if Adam and Eve had not sinned, this man still would have been born blind, because his blindness had a purpose to it and it was something good that he should have this state.

All human beings were made as good. But, because of original sin, we desired things that were bad and we suffered, even though we were not designed to suffer.

Now, here is something I will also state as an opinion, but something I have more certainty about than the one above: the body that Adam and Eve had before the fall and after was the same body, speaking biologically that is. The cells, the brain, the nerves, the muscles- all would be identical both before and after their sin.

I feel more certain of this, because the bodies we have are a product of evolution, and the animals also have aging, they also require sleep and food for survival, and other things we think of as deficiencies which are part of their biology. I don't think Adam and Eve experienced death was because God changed their genes and allowed them to age, I think it is rather He created them to age in the first place, but He had a way that they could live with these bodies forever through something God would provide them with (eg. perhaps like some kind of a medicine that could be made or other things that exist in the Creation).

People would be dependent on this thing in the Creation for living forever, just as Adam and Eve were dependent on the Creation to provide them with food for their bodies. And living close to God, they would have no difficulty in acquiring these things that their body needed to remain healthy and happy. Whether this was food, drink, shelter, medicine or even what could cure their aging— all was available to them with what God created, and if they had remained as they were, they would have had it.

But once they lost this relationship with Him, He allowed them to live without the things that their bodies and health needed. This included sufficient food, sufficient shelter, clean water, and all other human needs, and it would also perhaps have included whatever it was that was needed to cure their aging. The punishment of original sin was to keep paradise from Adam and Eve and their descendants, so that they were lacking the things that they were designed to have and which they needed to have in order to live healthy and happy lives without suffering or death.

And we today, still suffering the consequences of this sin still have to endure an existence where we lack things that we need, including what we need to cure our aging.

Adam and Eve would have had bodies designed for surviving by eating food both before and after the fall. The difference is that before the fall, they would have never been lacking in food that they needed. I speculate the same is true of aging. God didn't change their bodies, He simply just cut off what they needed to live forever without suffering and death.

They would have this aging process in their flesh, whether they ate the fruit or not, and this process was a good thing that glorified God; it was a reminder in the physical world that without Him, people could not have eternal life. Similarly, every other seeming deficiency that people are born with is just the same as this.

The biology was completely the same, this was not altered by the effects of the original sin; it is rather the relationship that was lost.

The problem was that they were designed for paradise, and they no longer lived in paradise. So, their bodies no longer functioned the way that they were supposed to, because they lost the relationship with the Person who provided for them.

People desire vengeance not because they were made bad, but because they were made good. What they really want is not vengeance, but justice. However, because they do not live in paradise, therefore the world doesn't have justice and their desire for justice is left without satisfaction. And so, the devil comes and the evil spirits come and present vengeance to human beings, telling them that this is the way that their desire can be satisfied, and it looks like justice and so people do desire it and they go out and commit vengeance. Their desires are in fact perfect. However, it was not for vengeance that they were created to desire, but it was justice that they were designed to desire.

Like a hungry man who has no food and so he desires to eat garbage because the garbage looks like food, the human being is like this in his exile from the garden.

People desire heresy, not because they were made bad, but because they were made good. They don't want heresy, but rather they want to believe in things that are more comfortable for them to believe. However, because they do not live in paradise, the Truth is something which is uncomfortable, something which does not always feel good, and so they desire heresy. What they really want is not heresy, but rather to live in a world where the Truth always is comfortable and feels good to believe in. And in paradise they can have that, but not here. Their desires are not wrong; what they desire is the state in paradise, but because they do not have paradise, therefore the heresy seems more appealing to their desires. It is not their desires, which are wrong, however; they are just not living in the place they were designed to live in.

People desire to steal, not because they were made bad, but because they were made good. They don't really want to steal, but they want to live in a world where they can have a nicer material existence than they do. However, because they do not live in paradise, they have to work in suffering for their daily bread. They do not desire to do this, because they were not designed for this, not because they are bad. They were designed to live in a world where work would have no suffering and no material need would ever be lacking, and their desires were designed for that world, not for this one. Hence, because you take something designed for paradise and put it in this world, therefore stealing becomes attractive, because it looks like it is the way to get the state that you were designed to live in and which your desires are made for.

The person who desires to be better than others possesses a desire given by God for the eternal glory in heaven, but because this person doesn't have this, this good desire for glory is in then transformed into a desire for human glory and surpassing other people. The desire is still part of who the person is, it doesn't need to be rejected, but it just needs to be understood better.

There is not really any such thing as an evil desire. All desires that people have are good and no one should reject their desires. But rather they have to change their understanding and realize that the things that they think they desire are not actually the things that they truly desire; they are seemingly wanting to eat garbage because they don't know about the real food.

Original sin did not change the human being at all. It took something that was perfect and it denied him the way to fulfill his every desire, and thus temptation therefore became attractive. Every moment of the life of a human being they will desire evil, not because there is anything wrong with their desires at all, but because they were designed for paradise and evil looks like the paradise they were designed for.

Every desire you can think of, no matter how perverse or atrocious it may seem, is still ultimately a desire for something in the paradise, but which is lacking in this world and it can't be given to human beings, because of sin that began with the fruit.

If I took a baby and put him into a world where he never suffered anything at all. Every desire was fulfilled, not according to what he wanted, but according to what actually fulfilled the desire and left him in peace. This child would grow up and think like an angel, because he would never learn to be selfish, since this trait is learned in order for the person to protect himself, and without the need, the trait is not developed. His psychology would lead him to think of others just as important as himself, and he would feel no threat from accepting this completely, and if he was raised like this in this setting, it would be completely instinctive to him, since accepting this would never mean that he didn't have what he wanted.

It is rather because people are missing things, that they develop a psychological selfishness. The person psychologically comes to develop the mindset that they have to seek their own interests over the interests of others, otherwise they will not have what they desire.

The human being is completely perfect in how he was created. He seeks after evil, because he was designed for paradise, and he can't have paradise because his ancestors ate the fruit and could not leave it as an inheritance to him.

You or I, would think and act just like Jesus and Mary, with the bodies and personalities we have, if we had been born into a world like that. And those two are like that, even though they were born into a world like this, because they never lost faith in God's love, but we did.

But there is no way to take a person and raise him like this. Because only God can completely fulfill the person's every need. If you gave the person everything they desired, they would still be selfish, because what they desire is not what they truly desire, and they will still be left hungry and will develop the same psychological traits of selfishness to protect their own needs as the rest of humanity.

If, however, from the moment they were born, they had everything that fulfilled their every need, because God gave them this grace, then they would never develop any psychological tendency to selfishness. You or I, or the rest of the human race are all like this – we would all be like angels in our hearts had it not been for the loss of paradise.

The bodies that human beings had would be identical both before and after the fall. All that changed was that the things that satisfied them were no longer there and instead temptation seemed like the only thing that could satisfy these desires for paradise that never went away.

The human being is so lustful, so insatiable, so absolutely craving of having everything– not because there is anything wrong with him at all, but because he was in fact designed to have God and thus having absolutely everything. But as long as he cannot have Him, he will crave evil instead with unlimited lusts, because the evil thing is here in front of him and it resembles the good thing he was designed for, which cannot be given him at present because sin exists.

He wants evil every day of his life, because he was designed to desire good, and the evil is the only thing in front of his eyes that looks like the good he was designed to desire.

Hence, I think this is partly why it was that Jesus told the disciples it was not because this man or his parents had sinned, which caused this. If Adam and Eve had not eaten the fruit, this man would still have been born blind in Eden. So also would every other deformity that comes from birth continue to exist.

However, people would be born with these things, and would not suffer even the tiniest bit as a result of these conditions. Adam and Eve would have the same bodies and they wouldn't die, not because their biology changed, but because whatever was needed to prevent their flesh from aging and suffering would have been given to it, just as the food that they needed to never starve would always be provided them or just as the water they needed to never thirst would always be provided them. The body that was capable of starving, thirsting or aging, however, would be the same.

The person with cystic fibrosis would have the gene problem and yet receive whatever it is in the creation they needed to have this body and suffer nothing at all in this condition. The person with wisdom teeth that gave him pain would never feel pain from these teeth, because whatever was needed to make this person have these teeth without any suffering anything would have been given to him.

Today we have medicines that can cure all kinds of diseases that were incurable in times past and these medicines come from the creation. If Adam and Eve had never sinned, whatever was in the creation that was needed in order for people to be born with the bodies they have and yet not suffer or die, would be given to them by God.

The answer to every biological problem was found somewhere in the creation, because all these things were made good and human beings were designed to live in the creation in perfect happiness. However, because of sin, this could not be given to them.

As the book of Wisdom says, God did not create death and there is no destructive poison in the Creation.

I do not think that Eden was a specific physical place, but rather Eden was simply the created world (ie. the Earth, the place we live in now) before they ate the fruit. They would have had the same bodies and lived in the same world as exists now, and not have suffered or died at all, because whatever was in the world that could allow them to enjoy such a state of permanent happiness would be arranged by God to come to them.

Somehow, the man would be born blind, and yet he would be perfectly happy like this and his condition would be used to both glorify God and love human beings. The same is true of any other deformity that a person is born with.

Someday, the person would be able to enjoy sight as well, to enjoy the state of the body without these deformities as well. But they never would have been unhappy for a moment to have had these deformities, and in fact people would not even label them as 'deformities' but simply as different ways of being human, because deformity would indicate that there was something bad about being this way, when the reality was that they did not suffer at all in having these conditions and these conditions were glorifying God.

The church teaches that we cannot reject the body we are created with. If a person is born blind, or born with a deformity, then they have to accept that body, because it is their body. It doesn't mean that they will never enjoy sight or never enjoy the condition of the body without the deformity - they will. It doesn't mean you can't do anything to help the person with their body to enjoy a better life- you can. But it is to say that this is part of who they are and part of the identity that God gave to them present in their bodies.

And I think, but cannot state for certain, that in the resurrection both the deformity and the condition of the body without the deformity would belong to the person forever.

But with homosexuality this is impossible. If people are homosexual because of the biology they are born with, then that would mean that they have to accept this, just as any other person must accept the body they are created with. To reject it, would be to commit sin.

Even if we say that homosexuality is a deformity, deformities are still part of who you are. We do not tell the person with Down syndrome, 'your brain is wrong, your personality is wrong, and you should reject these things and accept that you are something different'. A deformed brain is still his brain, a deformed personality is still his personality, and rejecting it as a sin against the first commandment.

With homosexuality, this is impossible for it to be a deformity. We can never say that homosexuality is part of a person, because it would fundamentally contradict what is understood about how God made the human being in His image, and reflecting the divine marriage in heaven.

The catechism teaches that homosexuality is a disordered condition, and it also teaches that each person must accept his or her sexual identity, and his or her body. You put these two together, it means that it is impossible for a person to be homosexual because of biology, for otherwise that would mean that you would have to reject the body given by God, which itself is a sin.

It is possible for God to design someone to be born blind, to be born without arms, to be born in any sort of way that seemed to human beings like it was a deformity, when in actuality it was just a different way of glorifying God. But it is impossible for him to design someone to be homosexual.

Hence, it is impossible that someone was homosexual from biology. If I am wrong about what I wrote above, and the fall of man from Adam and Eve really did change the body and made us different than what we were supposed to be, and none of those deformities could exist without the fall, then yes, it is absolutely possible for someone to be born homosexual because of their biology they are born with.

But I don't think it worked like this. I say this, because if it were like that then the church's teaching to tell people to accept the body they are given would not make sense, since we are then claiming that the body we are given can be wrong. If it can be wrong on this point, then why could we not also say it was wrong about every other thing that people felt uncomfortable with accepting?

The prohibition against mutilation would be meaningless, because mutilation is only a sin because you are rejecting the body God gave to you, but if this is true, then that is not actually the case and perhaps this thing you mutilate wasn't the body God gave to you.

If we say that the person with Down syndrome has this
because it is a flaw, or the person without eyes has this
because it is a flaw, and it wasn't God's will, then
that means that the body you are born with can be
wrong and not something from God, and therefore why
would we forbid mutilation? If the body isn't from
God, then mutilation isn't a sin.

But Genesis says that God made human beings as good,
and if the body is bad, then that means it is not from
God. The book of Wisdom says that there is no
destructive poison in what God created and that God
did not create death. But if people are born with
biological flaws, then that means there is destructive
poison in the creation.

The body is perfect. The body of the human being now
in this world is perfect. It is not the case that the body is
wrong or the human being is wrong, but it is rather the
case that he, who was made perfect, is not living in the
state he was designed to live in and so he has trouble
seeing how his body could be perfect.

The body with Down syndrome, the body born without
eyes, the body born without limbs— they are all perfect,
and in Eden the person who had this condition would
live in complete happiness with it. And this being true
would not mean (at least in my thinking, but I do not
know for sure) that the person could never enjoy, either
in this life or in the resurrection, the state of the body
without the Down syndrome, with the eyes or with the

limbs.

Human sexuality is really a very special topic, however.

Teresa of Avila famously once had an experience where an angel rammed a fiery spear into her body; it is called 'The Ecstasy of St Teresa'. In describing it, she wrote:

I saw in his hand a long spear of gold, and at the iron's point there seemed to be a little fire. He appeared to me to be thrusting it at times into my heart, and to pierce my very entrails; when he drew it out, he seemed to draw them out also, and to leave me all on fire with a great love of God. The pain was so great, that it made me moan; and yet so surpassing was the sweetness of this excessive pain, that I could not wish to be rid of it. The soul is satisfied now with nothing less than God. The pain is not bodily, but spiritual; though the body has its share in it. It is a caressing of love so sweet which now takes place between the soul and God, that I pray God of His goodness to make him experience it who may think that I am lying.[1]

In the gospel, Jesus says that in the resurrection, people neither marry nor are given in marriage, but they are like the angels in heaven.

---

[1] From Wikipedia page Ecstasy of Saint Teresa

Does this mean people who were spouses will not be spouses anymore and no longer have the same love for each other? I think the answer to that is yes and no. It is yes, because in heaven there will be a new relationship surpassing the old one, and a new everything surpassing the old everything, but it is also no, because there is nothing that the person had on Earth which they will not also have in heaven in a glorious form. Whatever was good in the relationship between a husband and wife on Earth, they will still have in heaven, but they will no longer have sexual relations. Their sexualities will be part of them forever, but they will not use them for marital sex any longer, instead they will be used for something even greater.

Joseph and Mary were never really a husband and wife on Earth, because they had no sexual relations. It is possible that they were a sign of what married couples will look like if they meet again in heaven, although what exactly this will be like, I again must confess that I don't know and it is a mystery which is not fully revealed to us, I think.

Human sexuality, which only could licitly take place in marriage will have to be ended, if in fact marriage no longer exists. But does that mean that people cannot have that feeling anymore? That the pleasure of sexuality cannot take place anymore?

What will this look like? - I point to Teresa as our example, perhaps.

Teresa was a woman, whose femininity reflected the Bride in the marriage that takes place in heaven. A woman is penetrated by her husband in the sexual act, and so Teresa was penetrated by the angelic spear. Whatever Teresa had in her own sexuality: feeling pleasure and pain in sex, feeling an emptying of self in sex, feeling the sweetness of the man's love in sex— she feels all these things that she could have felt with a man in the sexual act, and instead feels them with God — the angel acts as His agent. She is in the place of the bride to the bridegroom, experiencing in her consciousness an intense pleasure at being penetrated and filled with the love of God.

Human sexuality, both masculine and feminine, are reflections of the marriage in heaven. Every type of sexual feeling is included in this. Each sexual desire that a person may have has a corresponding meaning in this marriage in heaven.

What Teresa here has is the original, and the sexual act between men and women on Earth is the copy of the original, because human beings are made in God's image, not the other way around.

Our sexualities at the moment are just a shadow, and we will not see the full meaning of them until we get to God and are united to Him in heaven, as the bride is united with the bridegroom to become 'one flesh'.

Every bit of pleasure that a person was capable of feeling in their sexuality on Earth will not be lost in heaven, but rather it will be transformed. Marriage will not exist anymore, and therefore people will not have sex with one another anymore. But this union with God will replace this.

The sex between married couples is replaced with the union of God and human being. Nothing of the good that people had in life will be lost, but it will be transformed. Teresa᾽s experience is just a tiny clue as to what it will look like, but I think it is still very mysterious to us, we don't know how exactly this is going to be.

I wonder even if perhaps it could be like this, that the people who were married on Earth will both enjoy the ecstasy of the love of God together forever, and this is the way they are united with God in paradise, while someone like Teresa who was a nun in life and married to Jesus, has an experience like this instead with the angel. While someone who was a male who was celibate for the sake of the kingdom could have such an experience of ecstasy while giving his love to the church to whom he serves as a husband towards.

She in the place of the bride, and he in the place of the bridegroom, while people who chose to be married for the sake of the kingdom will instead have it together.

Nothing good is going to be lost; marriage will not exist, but nothing good will be lost- this is a mystery, and I am only offering a potential explanation of how that will happen.

But in all of this you also see an explanation for human sexual lusts. The human being has so much sexual lust, is not because there is anything wrong with his body at all. His brain is rather just seeking after a feeling of intense pleasure, but he has never had this thing that Teresa experienced, and the only place he knows where he can get such pleasure is in sexuality. Like a hungry man desiring to eat garbage, a human being who is denied this union with God then intensely desires sexuality, because the copy looks like the original and he has never even seen or heard of the original.

There is nothing wrong with him at all; he was perfect in his creation. He just doesn' t understand that the answer to his desires is this. People would not be lusting so much after sexual things if they had this union with God, because what they are really desiring is this union, but on Earth all they can see is sexuality and so they think they desire that.

So, this second possibility is impossible so far as Catholic teaching is concerned. Because homosexuality is disordered, it is impossible that someone is disordered in paradise. What your body had on Earth, you will also have in paradise, and it is impossible to be disordered in paradise. Hence, it cannot be possible that the disorder is in the body itself.

If a person has sexual desires for the same-sex because of the design of the biology, then that means the body you have is not the one that God gave you. And if that is true, then the prohibition against mutilation makes no sense either. Nor does what the church say about how a person must accept his or her own body make any sense.

I don't think this is possible, and the catechism in fact assumes it is psychological and not biological causes.

Therefore, that seems to leave us with the first possibility only.

It means that the gay person was born straight and developed a same-sex attraction due to environment or psychology, gets to heaven and finds as well as sees clearly that it was the opposite sex that was the answer to his desires all along, and he was simply confused in life due to a psychological environment that made him see the same sex as though it was the opposite sex.

There is nothing he loses that he had in life, all the homosexual nature he had (or rather 'seemed to have') will still exist, he will still be the same person as he was in life, but he will find that his desires were actually for a woman all along, and he just didn't realize it. The thing in his fantasies was always a woman, but it just looked like a man to him, because he was confused. He always was desiring a woman, he was never gay, but a man just looked like a woman to him, because the devil was allowed to manipulate his psychology like this, but the biology, the brain, and desire itself was never wrong.

There was nothing wrong with how he was created, there was nothing wrong in his desires or his nature; he just wasn't living in paradise, and therefore the evil looked to him like the good he was designed to desire.

3)   Hidden Gender

Now, I am not finishing here, however. It may seem like the debate is then closed on the question of whether one is born gay or not, but actually there is something else... There is yet another possibility which needs to be considered.

I think this explanation is going to be very hard for people in the church and many religions in general to accept, but I state in sincerity that it does not violate any doctrine of the church and is wholly in conformity with it.

This explanation I put forward as a possibility. However, there is still a fourth explanation after this which I personally find more likely.

The problem with rejecting a biological origin to homosexuality is that there is some degree of evidence pointing to a possible biological origin. And if this evidence proves true, then we are then left in a very tricky situation as far as Catholic doctrine is concerned, because it would seem to mean that there were in fact human beings whose genders were not made in the image of this divine marriage in heaven.

Now, suppose that scientists show in fact that it is actually true that there are people who are born with a neural biology that is designed to make them gay. We can't say that the body is wrong, because that would contradict what the church teaches about how we have to accept the body God gave to us. We also can't say that a person was designed to be gay, because that would contradict what we know about men and women being designed to mirror the marriage in heaven.

And furthermore, we can't just cover our eyes and plug our ears, and pretend like they are not discovering what they are discovering either.

The brain is a very complex organ and its mysteries are still far from being understood by us human beings.

Several years ago, there was a Welshman named Chris Birch who appeared in the news. He had been a beer-drinking rugby player who was engaged to his fiancée and lived a normal heterosexual life. He went mountain climbing and he had a stroke while climbing. The stroke briefly cut off the flow of blood to his brain, and as often happens in this situation, part of his brain was damaged by it. Some of the neurons die from lack of oxygen and the surviving neurons 'take over'.

He woke up from the stroke and found that he was different. He was no longer attracted to women, but instead had sexual desires for men. He lost interest in many of the things he liked before, and he changed his career to become a hair stylist. He got a boyfriend and lived an active gay lifestyle.

It is said that most people only use a small part of their brain for most of their lives. This means that they actually have large areas in their brain, which are capable of feelings and behaviours that they generally do not experience much in their lives, because these areas are unused.

Like muscles that we never exercise, there are supposedly large parts of our brain that we don't use and we have much greater intellectual capacity than we would think, but we just don't use those parts. After a stroke, however, the body is forced to change the parts of the brain that are used because some parts are killed and other parts need to take over.

And if a part that we use the most is killed by the stroke, then we start using the parts we didn't use, and it will seem like our personality then changes, but actually we are just using a part of ourselves that we didn＇t know was there before. And alternatively, if the part that isn＇t used much is killed by the stroke, it will seem like we are still the same person and have just as much intellect as we did before, even though we technically only have half a brain now.

For those who assert that homosexuality results from psychology, they have to deal with this sort of evidence and cases like this and ask the question: did this happen to Chris because of an absent father figure or an upsetting of the gender environment he was raised in? Is it because he had an immature personality and hadn＇t passed certain stages in his psychological development? Is it because he had older brothers who bullied him and scared him of being masculine, and so he didn＇t properly form his own gender identity? Are we sure this really wasn＇t because of neural biology?

It is possible that he is just completely lying and it was all just a huge elaborate act put on for years in front of his family, friends and fiancée, with the stroke being planned beforehand as the moment he chose to do the switch in his life, but it is a sin to assume such a thing about a person without knowledge. It is also possible that maybe he did have homosexual feeling before the stroke and just isn't telling the truth about it, and the stroke didn't actually change this, but again it is a sin to assume the person is lying without evidence.

Theoretically, assuming he is not lying, the part of the brain that gave Chris these homosexual feelings would have theoretically been there the whole time, but he just hadn't used it before the stroke killed part of the brain he was using and forced him to use part he was not using.

And scientists are debating this question and publishing contradictory conclusions on the topic. Generally, there is some amount of consensus that the brains of active homosexuals and the brains of active heterosexuals appears to illustrate some differences. One study claimed that lesbian woman had a higher tendency of blinking when they heard a crashing noise than heterosexual woman, which suggests a difference in the nervous system (ie. the brain) which causes the person to make the automatic reaction. Men are more likely to blink when hearing a crashing noise than women. Perhaps it is an evolutionary thing that came from the time when people were cavemen and men would go out hunting big animals. Such an automatic and instinctive neural reaction perhaps could protect the eyes of the hunter. There has been evidence published that show lesbian women also share this blinking tendency with heterosexual men.

Furthermore, certain parts of the brains of some homosexual men have shown a certain resemblance with the brains of heterosexual females rather than with heterosexual men.

Neural science is not very well developed at our point in history, however. To say that they see differences between the brains does not mean that they understand why these differences exist or what the differences do.

Two hundred years ago, during the pioneer days of geology, geologists could have stated that it appeared like layers of rock formed in strata, and some geologists speculated that the Earth could have been far older than the bible's chronology, although it took a long time before this could be proven as anything more than just a theory. They did not yet know about radiometric dating, evolutionary biology or other things that needed explanations to put the Earth's history together, and in the end, they found that it did in fact refute the narrative believed by Christians following the genesis narrative about the young Earth. Our current research on the brain could be something similar.

For one thing, to find differences between the brains does not even denote a cause-effect relationship. For example, it could be the case the differences are caused by the behaviour itself, meaning that a person in a homosexual relationship will have changes in their brain that are different than what happens in the heterosexual's brain, and that the change observed in the brain is an effect of the behaviour, and not the cause of the attraction.

Studies have been done on twins, where it was found that when an identical twin was gay, the likelihood of the other twin also being gay was only 10 to 20 percent, which suggests that at least it was not genes that was the sole determining factor.

Studies have done showing correlations between development of homosexual tendencies and experiences in childhood, especially with abuse. It has been reported that children raised by homosexuals have a much higher tendency of themselves developing such tendencies than children not raised by homosexuals – which again fits very well at establishing the nurture rather than nature.

But such studies are not conclusive enough to prove the claim that no one is born with a homosexual disposition. Neural science still remains in its infancy and scientists will have a lot of work to do before they can prove these theories as necessarily true.

For me, this is ultimately a debate that has to be left to scientists, however.

But, assuming it is from neurological causes, how do I explain this?

Let me try my best.

Gender is given by God at the moment a person is conceived, and it is permanently a part of who the person is. The catechism teaches that every person must accept the sexual identity given to them by God.

Now, which part of the body is it that determines gender?

This might seem like a silly question, but it is not. The answer is not as obvious as you may think.

Did you know that there are women who are born with 100% male DNA?

All foetuses, male or female, begin in the womb with female bodies. The female is the default state of the foetus. But during the pregnancy, hormones will be triggered by the DNA of the foetus such that if it is a boy, then a hormone will enter which will cause the brain to change, and the body to develop male attributes. If this hormone does not enter, because there is a gene malfunction or some other cause that prevents it from being accepted by the foetus, then the foetus continues to develop as a female even though the DNA is male.

The person is then born with a female body and a female brain, but because of the male DNA, they are born without ovaries or a uterus, and they have internal testes and their vagina ends in a pouch. They are incapable of bearing children and they don't have periods. It is a very rare condition, but it is a proven biological reality. A famous example of an XY woman is the American actress Eden Atwood.

There is another real and proven medical condition where a person is born with male DNA and has a woman's body at birth, possessing a vagina but with internal male sex organs. However, when the person reaches puberty, they develop as a male, the voice lowers, they start growing facial hair, etc.

There are people born with XX(female) DNA and develop male exterior characteristics, with a penis, facial hair at puberty, etc. but yet possess ovaries and a uterus Inside. It is extremely rare, but it does exist.

And so, you see, it is not as black and white as we may like to assume.

People will say that a man is a man and a woman is a woman, because the DNA is like this, because the sex organs are like this. But there are people who are quite clearly women who are born with testes and male DNA. The testes don't work, but there are normal men who are born with testes that don't work too.

And if the DNA and sex organs is not what marks the sex, then what do you use?

Suppose we just say that we will ignore the question of DNA and sex organs and say that whichever one develops the body as a man and whichever one develops the body as a woman, that one is a man or a woman. Whichever one has a body that looks like a male body (excepting the DNA and sex organs), that is a man, and whichever one has a body that looks like a female body （excepting the DNA and sex organs） that is a woman.

But again, as I already mentioned, there are some people in existence who do not develop their bodies in a normal way and because of some complication, they do not go through the developments in the body which are normal for other people, so the bodies they possess have DNA and characteristics that can be for either sex. Hence, it is not as simple as this.

As far as natural reason is concerned, wouldn't the most obvious part of the body to look at in this question be the brain?

If the gender is part of the soul of the individual, and the brain is linked with the thoughts and personality of the person, how could this not be the most obvious place in the body to determine the gender of the individual?

There are people who are born without sex organs, there are people born with deformed bodies that are unrecognizable as male or female, but there are never people who are born without brains. If we wanted to know the gender of the person as God gave to them, the gender of the soul, of all the parts of the body that could be chosen, the brain is the most obvious part of the body.

The women who have male DNA should be counted as women, not because of their exterior appearance, but because their brains are female brains.

Whether or not there are males who are born with female brains or feminized brains, I am not of sufficient scientific authority to write about this, although there are people arguing in this debate just as they are over the question of whether homosexuality is biological or not.

However, if the brain is in fact the part of the body that ultimately defines the gender of the person, we have to then split hairs even further and ask 'what part of the brain is it that causes a person to have one gender over another?'

Because, perhaps a brain could be formed in a person which was neither a normal male nor normal female brain, but something different, and therefore how could you judge the gender of it?

We put the conclusions together we can find our answer. If God creates no one as gay, and no one could be gay because of their biology, then it must be the case that if someone has a same sex attraction and this comes from the neural biology God gave to them, then this person in question must be counted as a member of the opposite sex.

As John Paul II said when speaking of Galileo, whom the church persecuted even though he was right: 'truth cannot contradict truth'. Catholic doctrine is true, and science is true, but somehow, they must both be true without contradicting.

That is to say, if a boy is born gay, and this really is part of him biologically, then he is actually a girl and not a boy, even if everything else about him is as a boy and his brain, while possessing a difference from heterosexual males, is still not the same as the brain that women have.

He may have the personality of a male, he may think like a male, have interests like a male and behave like a male. But if his sexual orientation is towards males and this is because of the brain he was born with, then he is to be counted as a woman and not a man. He possesses a female soul and he was designed for men.

His sexual identity reflects the Bride and not the

Bridegroom.

And the gay woman, vice-versa.

Perhaps there is a mystery in this in that the Bride contains both men and women, and so the existence of the gay male, who is a woman that is otherwise masculine, is like a reflection of the men who are in the church and thus form the Bride. While the feminine characteristics of God (the bible uses feminine characteristics to describe God at times) are reflected by the existence of the gay woman, who is otherwise feminine, but in fact possesses a masculine soul and reflects the Bridegroom.

It also perhaps points to the mystery of all the people in other religions who were actually seeking God, even though they had not yet received the gospel. Even though it appeared like the people were seeking created idols and God was not marrying them, they were actually seeking Him and He was putting seeds in their culture to follow. Even though it appeared like the Bride was marrying the Bride and the Bridegroom was marrying the Bridegroom, in actuality the Bride was marrying the Bridegroom and it was all just disguised.

The Bride is not just those in the church, but it is also these people who I wrote are catechumens that have not yet entered the church and die before reaching it; similarly, femininity is not just those who are born with female bodies, but it is also including these males who are born with brains that design them sexually for other males.

The Bridegroom is not just the God who speaks to the church, but it is also the God who speaks to all people throughout the creation, including those who have not yet heard the gospel preached to them and who will die without receiving it; similarly, masculinity is not just those who are born with male bodies, but it is also including those females who are born with brains that design them sexually for other females.

And thus, they can reflect the mystery of God and the marriage in heaven. The doctrinal obstacle is then solved.

There is no Catholic doctrine being broken here. No one is being created gay, the church's teachings about the person remains intact; their same-sex attractions are heterosexual attractions in disguise.

To anyone who claims this is heresy, I ask them to find any document or authoritative statement made from the magisterium in the past 2000 years that ever defined which part of the body it was that defined a person as man or woman. It does not exist; the church has never made such a statement, it has only said that homosexuality is a disordered condition.

If this third option is correct, homosexuality is still a disordered condition, and this is not actually homosexuality, but simply heterosexuality in disguise.

And the catechism's statement about being a disordered condition, would then no longer apply to them, since the attraction is not actually homosexual.

I suppose the authors of the catechism did not intend it to be interpreted like this, but I think the fathers at the Council of Florence in the 15th century did not intend their words to be interpreted the way we have interpreted it today either. Nothing is different. The question for us, as for all human beings, is whether we follow them, who were created, or the Person who speaks through them.

The ball then falls into the court of scientists. If they prove that homosexual attractions are from psychology only, then this option does not apply. If, however, they demonstrate that homosexual attractions do come from neural biology and there are in fact people born this way, then this is the option that would then follow.

If so, then the choice here is either the church is wrong, and people are in fact born gay, or the church is right and the people born gay were given souls of the opposite sex, which reflected the other side of the divine marriage in their own unique way.

The church teaches that the body cannot be rejected

and it must be accepted. Even when people have deformities, the deformities are still part of who they are. This is exactly why homosexuality cannot possibly be biological and if it is, then it must be heterosexual in disguise, because God makes no one gay.

Their souls are ultimately just as feminine or masculine as any normal male or female, even if their bodies or personalities are seemingly not. They may not feel comfortable thinking of themselves as members of the opposite sex either, because they have been raised and always thought of themselves as the sex they were seemingly born with. Furthermore, there is no reason why they would need to think of themselves as members of the opposite sex, cross-dress, behave differently or change anything about themselves either. To say that they are women in disguise, or they are men in disguise, does not mean that they are not the people they are now. They are who are they are, and if they were to try to change themselves to become someone different, they would be making a mistake.

Their male bodies are actually female bodies, but they look like male bodies. Their female bodies are actually male bodies, but they look like female bodies. Their male personalities are actually female personalities, but they seem like male personalities. Their female personalities are actually male personalities, but they seem like female personalities. Everything they are is a reflection of the gender of their soul, even though it is disguised.

They can (and ought to) continue being the people that they are- but it just has to be understood that God did not create them or anyone as a person with a same-sex attraction.

The pagan searches for the Truth in life and he is effectively a catechumen to a church he has not yet been baptized into. He cannot find God before baptism, but it is He who he is searching for and he is catechumen to Him. However, before he dies, in this world, he struggles and can' t worship the God he is searching for in the way he ought to, because he has not yet found Him except as an idea perceived through reason. But when he dies, he can find God and worship Him in spirit and truth.

Similarly, the man born gay is looking for a male partner, but it is impossible for him to find a true marriage with this partner in life, because without being open to procreation, sexual acts are illicit. And even if he is a female in disguise, his personality still is not designed in the same way as a normal female's personality is that make it easy for her to feel happy in a relationship with a male.

So, he struggles in this world, and cannot marry the person he is looking to marry; his existence doesn' t seem to make sense. He doesn't understand why God made him gay. But when he dies, he sees clearly what the answer was to why he was like this, and how it also reflected the mystery of the marriage in heaven.

The person looks like they are following a created religion, but actually they are catechumens listening to God's word as it is disguised in their culture and will find salvation. It looked like the bride was marrying the bride, but actually she was marrying the bridegroom, and it was just disguised. It looked like the bridegroom was marrying the bridegroom and enjoying heaven by Himself, but actually He was planting seeds in this pagan culture to court the love of His bride. So also, perhaps people are designed to be homosexual, but are not actually homosexual, because their gender is different from what it appears to be, and they are heterosexual in disguise.

We are created in God's image and by our genders we show this mystery of the marriage in heaven. It is perhaps possible that God designed people with hidden genders as one more aspect in which we reflect this marriage by the image imprinted upon us.

The man outside the church finds God in life and gets to heaven, even though it seemed like he was following something created, but in reality, he was also a catechumen to the church. The man with a female soul, looks like he is a man, but actually his personality and body in life was a reflection of his femininity.

Bisexuality could not truly exist either, if I am right about all of this. All of the sexual feelings that a person is capable of feeling must somehow have an ability to be satisfied within a heterosexual relationship. Whether it be fetishes, cross-dressing, submission or domination, desire for touching children, desire for rape, desire for sex with animals, desire for this kind of sex or that kind, somehow all these desires are actually for a heterosexual spouse and can be fully satisfied in the sexual act with a heterosexual spouse and people are under deception when they think this desire is meant to be satisfied in some sinful way. None of these feelings should be rejected, all should be accepted, but they must be understood that their true satisfaction is found in a heterosexual relationship.

What I meant by this is that the person who wants to rape someone, what they fantasize about is actually a wife, and the rape victim he dreams about is actually a wife, although because of psychological confusion he thinks it is a person who is forced against their will to have sex. The person who desires to touch children, the children that he daydreams about is actually a spouse he is married to, although because of psychological confusion, he thinks it is a child. And so on.

Similarly, bisexual people are actually only designed for one sex, and the desires they have for one sex are actually designed for a relationship with the other, but because of psychological confusion, it appears to the person to be otherwise.

If homosexuality was psychological it would also have to be like this, because it would mean that the other man he fantasizes about is actually a woman, but it seems like a man to him. None of the feelings should be rejected, all must be embraced. They must be embraced so deeply that the person realizes that what he thinks he wants is not good enough for him, and he must seek more than this, he must seek God.

A person who is bisexual must also be like this; all their feelings somehow are for a heterosexual relationship.

There is also another possibility for them, however. They perhaps could have been designed for relationships with the opposite sex and with those members of the same sex who are actually the opposite sex in disguise. In other words, for example, if a woman has bisexual feelings and desires women, the feelings she has could perhaps be designed for women who have male souls, and thus her attraction is still ultimately a heterosexual one.

There is no one in existence who is not heterosexual. All forms of human sexuality are all heterosexual and designed to be satisfied within a marital act, whether it be the copy on earth or the divine union in heaven, but people can be confused about it because original sin makes it seem like the only way to fulfill these good desires is for something which is bad.

Psychology is warped by original sin, because human beings are designed for paradise, and when they do not have it, they do not think and feel the way they were designed to think and feel. Every sexual desire is designed for fulfillment by a spouse (whether in the copy on Earth or the original marriage in heaven) within a heterosexual relationship, and before the fall from grace, it would have been thus fulfilled.

4) Combination

The third possibility, however, is not the explanation that I personally find most convincing.

I am not certain which explanation of these four is the true one, in fact, although the fourth explanation, which I will present here, is the one that makes the most sense to me, although this explanation could be mistaken.

The only explanation, which I rule out as possible is the second one, because my understanding of Catholic doctrine is that rejecting the body is rejecting the Creator, and if you say that homosexuality is from biology (and it is not heterosexuality in disguise) then this is incompatible with the truth concerning our genders being a reflection of the marriage in heaven.

The fourth explanation is a combination of the first and the third. That is to say, there are some people who have homosexual feelings because of biology (and thus they are actually the opposite sex in disguise, like how the person outside the church who is seeking the Truth is still like the Bride in disguise), and at the same time there also some people who have homosexual feelings, not because they were born like this, but because their psychologies have been warped by their environment such that they have developed such attractions, but their sexuality remains designed for the opposite sex.

That is to say, there are people who are born with brains that design them to be heterosexual, but as a result of psychological environment post-birth, their feelings find satisfaction in the same sex rather than the opposite sex, even though they were designed for the opposite sex.

At the same time, there are also people who are born with brains that design them to be homosexual, and when they reach puberty, they develop as they were designed to develop and have hardwired homosexual attractions. This attraction is part of their identity, but only as a heterosexual one in disguise and not truly as a homosexual one, because no one was created as homosexual.

If people tell the person born heterosexual to accept himself as homosexual, then they are harming the person. Similarly, if they tell the person born homosexual who was in fact created this way to reject himself and believe he was designed for the opposite sex, then they are also harming the person. Since in either case they are asking the person to go against God's plan in their design.

And perhaps they will even fight each other, because they assume they are the same and don't understand that they are different. That is to say, the person born homosexual will try to get the person born heterosexual to accept himself as gay, and make him think that he really is born like this and will never be free of these feelings. At the same time, the person born heterosexual will try to convince the person born homosexual that it is in fact possible to change and get over these feelings, and he must stop thinking that God made him this way.

There have been numerous scientific studies which have offered evidence against the idea that a person is born homosexual. I mentioned this above already.

As I mentioned, there is a lot of evidence out there pointing to higher rates of people developing homosexual attractions in linkage to experiences of abuse as children or when they are raised by homosexuals.

Now, this evidence, while it must be admitted if genuine, has a flaw in it.

Firstly, to say that there is a higher likelihood of developing homosexual attractions after such experiences as children, does not actually completely refute the idea that homosexuality could be biological.

I mentioned earlier that findings showing a difference in brains between homosexuals and heterosexuals does not actually mean that this change didn't result from the behaviour rather than being the cause of the behaviour. The environment of the person and his own lifestyle will affect his own brain's development.

If you are able to follow the logic to its natural end, then you can then make sense of where the flaw is in the evidence of linking childhood experiences to homosexual behaviour. The flaw is that this evidence is being used to assert that the attraction is from psychology and not from biology, but as we just mentioned, the lived experiences are able to alter the biology. If we find that it is more likely for a person to be homosexual if they are raised by homosexuals or if they have certain childhood experiences, does that actually show that the person doesn't have the attraction because it is hard-wired into the brain- seeing that the brain itself and how it developed at that age could have been affected by such experiences?

Maybe it was the case that had the experiences not have happened, the person would not have developed the attraction, but that doesn't seem to prove the point that the attraction doesn't come from the development of the brain itself.

If a person was abused as a child, and this caused the brain itself to develop in such a way as to have a sexual attraction to the same sex, then homosexuality for him is still biological and not psychological.

There's a second flaw as well, and a far more critical one, but I want to address this after I point out the twin study.

Studies have been done on identical twins, who are genetically the same, and where one twin is gay. And these studies have found results such as that maybe 90% of the time, the other twin is not gay, while 10% of the time the other twin is gay, which is then put forward as evidence that the homosexual attraction is not innate.

While not being a scientist, I feel I could critique this too, however.

Firstly, while not delving too deeply into the science of which I can't claim expertise, I do know enough to state that to prove that homosexuality is not genetic and to say it is not biological are two different things. Twins have different fingerprints as well, even though their DNA is identical. Genes are not the only contributing factor that controls the development of the physical biology; like Eden Atwood, it is in fact possible to have 100% male DNA and not even be male, because the hormones control the biological development. Hence, even if there is no 'gay gene' that still doesn't mean the person can't be born with a biological homosexuality.

Secondly, when you have families where one sibling is gay (and they are not twins), is it a 10% likelihood that the other sibling will be gay as well? I don't know the answer to the question, but I've never seen anything written about this that seemed to present any investigation into that question, however, the question would need to be answered in the affirmative, otherwise the argument about the twin study could actually be seen as supporting a genetic root to homosexuality rather than debunking it, seeing that when the siblings raised in the same environment didn't share the same DNA the homosexuality was less likely, but when they shared DNA it was more likely.

Now finally, there is a critical flaw in this science, which I feel is not being taken into account by those using the studies to argue in favour of religious doctrine.

That flaw essentially is: in order to prove that people are not born gay, you have to prove that all people everywhere are born straight and not even one can be born gay. If you simply present evidence that shows that most gay people are not born gay, that generally there seems little difference in the brains of gay and straight people, that generally there seems like a stronger case for psychological origins, etc. that doesn't do anything at producing the conclusion that <u>all</u> gay people are not born gay.

If 99% of gay people are born heterosexual, and because of environment, they develop a homosexual attraction, while 1% of gay people are born homosexual, and they develop a homosexual attraction, then the doctrine still has a serious and critical problem.

They are using these studies to back up religious doctrine, but what is not being understood here is that the religious doctrine requires that not even one, at any time, anywhere is born gay, or else the doctrine is false.

If we are able to present evidence that shows how people with homosexual attractions generally went towards heterosexual attractions in life, it ultimately doesn't do anything to disprove this possibility. If we showed that huge numbers of homosexuals had experiences in childhood that correlate to homosexuality, it doesn't do anything to disprove the possibility that someone could be born gay. Not a single one of these studies is able to demonstrate that.

Let me try to use a parallel example to try to

demonstrate this.

For a long time, it was assumed that Columbus was the first European to reach the Americas. In the 20th century, however, a Viking settlement was discovered on the island of Newfoundland in Canada, which thereby proved that the Vikings had come much earlier than Columbus. Although there are a few legends of others that have crossed even earlier (like Irish saints in the dark ages), there is no evidence that people seem to be able to find anywhere of an earlier crossing.

Now, is it right then to assume that an earlier crossing did not occur?

Historians may feel comfortable about assuming it, but as far as logic is concerned, it would be senseless to rule it out and say that it was impossible. As long as the naval technology that could have allowed for a crossing existed in earlier periods, then how could we ever know that there was never a person in the dark ages, in the time of the Roman empire, or even earlier, who made the crossing and just left no record for posterity? To say that we do not have evidence for it existing and to say that it doesn't exist are two different things. The former conclusion is correct, and the latter is flawed. If it were religious doctrine, however, it would require the latter to be true or else the doctrine can be doubted.

As long as we know that it was possible for them to cross with the technology and expertise they had, then it is not possible to rule it out, since we don't (and we never will) have complete assurance that such a crossing would have left something for the modern day to find.

Now, the critical flaw in the arguments against biological homosexuality is very similar to this. Since in order to make the conclusion being made, that nobody is born gay, you need to show that it is actually impossible for the brain to form in that way that would cause a person to develop such an attraction. Finding evidence that shows many homosexuals may have had attractions from non-biological factors does nothing to establish this conclusion being made, since the evidence does not actually fulfill the logical requirements of the hypothesis.

I think many scientists doing these experiments are running them in order to disprove the hypothesis that people can be born gay, which is being championed by other scientists. But really, in order to prove that homosexuality is not biological, simply showing that there are gay people that are not born gay is nowhere near enough; they have to prove that all gay persons at all times everywhere had these attractions from non-biological origins. To prove this, you would need to know far more about the brain itself and how it works than our time period in history presently knows.

But to say that homosexuality can be biological in origin,

you only need one person at one time who you can demonstrate had his attraction from biology rather than environment, and your case is then settled. But, of course, you have to prove that the attraction really did come from biology and not from environment. Anecdotes like Chris Birch can help serve here, but this is not enough.

If his attraction was because of the stroke, and not because of environment, then clearly biology can be the source of the attraction. But was the attraction he had after the stroke really designed for a man and not for a woman? This is harder to answer.

Of the possibilities in the list above, I find this one to be most compelling in explaining what has actually been happening in reality.

But I think it must have been this way; at least it makes sense to me, if we consider the people in other religions. Do all people who worship in other religions, follow the Truth and get to heaven? If they did, then the third possibility ought to be correct. But, if in fact most of them do not, because they are ultimately failing to follow the Truth, but a few of them are following the Truth and do get to heaven- then the fourth possibility ought to be the correct one.

Paul wrote 'what pagans offer to idols, they offer to

demons and not to God'; a creature engaging with a creature.

Both types exist, those who are homosexual because they were made this way (thus are heterosexual in disguise) and those who have same-sex attractions they were not designed to have.

It is a little bit similar to saying that in other religions outside the church, there are ways that people in other religions are seeking the Creator and ways they are seeking the creature, things that are true and good in other religions, and things that are evil and false in other religions.

If most people in other religions are following things that are false and not following the Truth, but some of them are even though it appears like they are not, then I think it makes sense why human sexuality should be like this if most homosexuals have the condition from psychology and not from biology.

If there are homosexual persons who give up the homosexual lifestyle and speak about the evils of it, how harmful it was and how they found they were not designed for this, they may be telling the complete truth, but it still doesn't mean that there was no one who was homosexual who was designed for a homosexual attraction, but this attraction, despite its semblances, was actually heterosexual in disguise.

If the people of the other religions stop following these false things, become baptized and reject their former religions, and testify about how false they were and how deceptive they were, what they say may be true, but it still doesn't mean that there was no one in those religions who was following the Truth and finding God even while seemingly following a created religion.

All human sexuality is a mirror of the spiritual reality between God and human beings.

All of those theories about how psychological environment transforms a heterosexual person into a homosexual one (or rather a person burdened with same-sex tendencies), may be true for many people. However, it might not be true for all people who have homosexual feelings.

It is dangerous for missionaries to simply assume that everything in the pagan culture and religion is to be rejected, because there may be much good in it as well. Similarly, it may be dangerous for the church to tell all people of homosexual feelings that they are disoriented and that they were meant to feel differently, because by doing so you may in fact be telling them to reject God's plan in their creation.

The church teaches that people must accept their sexual identity. It says this in the catechism. If a person is born with these feelings, then that means that they commit a sin by rejecting them, because they are then rejecting their sexual identity and violating church teaching. The clergy who wrote the catechism perhaps did not understand it like this, but that does not matter, because we as Catholics follow not them but the One who speaks through them.

When the Pope tells people not to reject their genders, and that we must have 'human ecology', this must also extend to telling people not to reject a homosexual attraction they were born with either. The Pope perhaps does not understand his own words like this, but that is not important, because it is not him that we follow but rather the One who speaks through him.

However, as I mentioned before, there is no magisterial document in existence that ever explained what part of the body it was that constituted a person being male or female, and the explanation I have provided is one that fits with natural reason if in fact we were to find that homosexuality was from neural biological causes for at least some people.

Now, there are strange ramifications to this, if it is true.

For example, if it is possible for a person to be born gay and a person to be born straight, as well as for a person to be born straight and have a same-sex attraction they were not designed for, so also it ought to be possible for a person to be born gay and yet because of psychological environment, they developed a heterosexual attraction they were not designed for.

Furthermore, such 'confused' homosexuals seeking heterosexual relations will also find a lack of true sexual complementarity in the relationship, because it is gay relationship in disguise.

Studies showing gay people moving from homosexuality towards heterosexuality over life, could in fact also be masking a psychological manipulation of the environment that programs people to be heterosexual, just like how environment could cause a heterosexual to develop a homosexual attraction.

If people can be psychologically manipulated to develop same-sex attractions, then a person who actually is born gay should be even easier to manipulate to develop an opposite sex attraction, because the normalcy of heterosexuality in every culture of the world is far more prevalent than the normalcy of homosexuality. Furthermore, it is also possible that a brain designed for a homosexual attraction may retain many things that make it easier to form a marital relationship with a person of the opposite sex, even if the brain is not designed to recognize the opposite sex as sexually attractive.

I said above that if salvation outside the church is

possible, then gay marriage is possible as well. We know that both are impossible, however. But the mystery of how the man finds salvation through the church, without even hearing a missionary, and who is not baptized until he dies, is very much like how the gay person can be truly made for a gay union, but cannot licitly be married until he gets to heaven and is united with God. But the person who seemingly finds salvation outside of the church, is still finding it within the church, because he is a catechumen to the words of the angels planted in his culture, and that Truth is the Truth of the church, while similarly the gay person is made for a gay union, but it is not actually a gay union, because he is the opposite sex in disguise.

Missionaries ought to embrace what is true in other cultures and other religions, while teaching them that Truth and salvation comes from Jesus Christ within the church. Similarly, the church should not tell homosexuals to reject their sexual identities if in fact they were born with it, but they must teach them not to seek a sexual relationship with another person but instead seek for the union in heaven with God.

Missionaries must be very careful to reject what is bad and embrace what is good in the pagan culture. Similarly, the church must be careful about this as well, to direct people born straight who develop homosexual feelings through their psychological development to recognize they are made straight, and to direct people born gay (who are not really gay at all, but heterosexual in disguise) to embrace their sexual identity as for the same-sex.

If this explanation is true, it will change nothing about the fact that sexual acts between members of the same sex are not permissible. Because even if the relationship is actually heterosexual in disguise, it still is not morally licit because sex cannot produce offspring.

If a normal heterosexual couple who are married cannot use contraceptives, cannot have full oral sex, full anal sex or have sex in any way that it is impossible to produce pregnancy, then obviously a heterosexual couple in disguise cannot do this either.

When the sacrament of marriage is given in the church, the priest explicitly asks the people 'will you accept children from the Lord?', and if the answer is no, he is not supposed to marry them. Hence, nothing of the above will change anything in the church practice on that particular point, since a gay couple, even should they be heterosexual in disguise, cannot produce children and thus the priest must not marry them.

This does, however, perhaps explain what I wrote earlier about sexual complementarity. Because, theoretically, if God does not make people gay, then they won't be designed for a gay relationship, and so if they try to have such a relationship, they themselves ought to find themselves miserable in the relationship after enough time has passed. The church should not even need to tell them that there is something wrong with the lifestyle, because they should find it miserable themselves.

And indeed, there are many gay persons who have found themselves miserable in such relationships and such lifestyles. However, at the same time, there seem to be others who endure in stable monogamous relationships for decades or even their whole lives and at least by appearances they seem to be happy, which is hard to understand if the sexual complementarity is not there, as I wrote above.

If they are heterosexual in disguise, and one of the partners is actually a member of the opposite sex, then they could be designed for each other, however, and the sexual complementarity could exist and the church teaching would not be broken.

Being born gay (should it be proven that this is a scientific reality) and the church's teaching on gender and the person, do not have to be contradictory. They do not need to contradict any more than did Galileo or Darwin's discoveries need to contradict the church's teaching about God's role in the creation of the universe and human life.

However, this ultimately has to be something that is left to the church to speak more about and for scientists to do better research on. There is nothing I have written above that contradicts the doctrines in any way, but I am not the church and I must insist that should the church reject this, I will reject it too.

Lord, we pray that you give clarity to us and to the church about your creation of men and women, and help us to stay clear of all forms of heresy or fundamentalism regarding this subject. We pray that all those with same-sex attractions will accept and embrace themselves in the way that you truly made them as heterosexual people, and help their true identities be reconciled with both themselves and the world they live in. We ask for these things, if it is your will, in Jesus' name, Amen

VII: A Flaw

There is one potential flaw, which stands to unravel all I

have written, which I need to point out here.

I've stated that all sexuality must somehow be designed for a heterosexual relationship, and even if a person has feelings for a child, an object, an animal, or someone of the same sex, somehow it must be the case that this attraction was something that was originally designed for use in a heterosexual relationship.

It is impossible to say that the biology itself causes the person to be designed for anything other than the opposite sex, because it is not possible to say that the body the person was given is wrong, and to claim such a thing about the biology would in essence be to say such a thing.

Now, suppose, however we were to find that the biology of a person really did design them in such a way that it was inclined towards something other than the opposite sex? If a person really was designed sexually for both sexes, or if a person really was designed sexually for an animal or for a child, how could this be reconciled with what was written above?

It could not be reconciled. In fact, if it were the case that such a person existed, then the entire theology concerning the sexes as being a replication of the divine marriage in heaven would then need to be called into question, as would the doctrine about human beings being made in God's image, as well as the doctrine that our bodies are perfect and do not contain flaws.

One of these would logically have to have an error in it, if in fact such a thing were to genuinely exist.

Either the divine marriage was not as we supposed it to be, and human beings who are designed for both sexes or for something other than another human, were reflecting God in a way that we perhaps don't comprehend at the moment.

Or, human beings being made in God's image did not mean that our sexualities were a reflection of Him and being made in His image did not mean that everything about us was made in His image, but in fact it meant something else.

Or, alternatively, our very flesh itself is no longer perfect as a result of original sin and it is then possible to say that our bodies are corrupted. The person whose flesh causes them to have such an attraction is somehow warped from what it was meant to be in God's original plan. And the belief that the bodies we are born with have to be embraced and accepted by us is then in fact false.

All three of these seem impossible to me, which is why I suspect that anyone who has a desire for such things is actually just possessing a desire intended for a heterosexual relationship somehow. But if people were to discover that such a thing did exist, that the desire of the person itself came from something designed for these things, then I think that one of these three possibilities would need to be true, otherwise the Catholic faith itself was not based on Truth.

Lord, we pray that you help theologians in the church to have a deeper understanding of these issues and to help keep them free from error. We pray that you help us to understand your plan in the creation of the human being as you desire it to be understood. We ask for these things, if it is your will, in Jesus' name, Amen

VIII: Possibilities and Impossibilities

Notwithstanding the above potential flaw, there are a number of ramifications that would still have be to considered if in fact people were born gay and thus were members of the opposite sex in disguise.

I have already explained that even should this be true, gay marriage is still impossible, homosexual activity still must be condemned and the church still doesn't accept that people are made gay.

There are some things in the church practice that would be affected by this, however.

If they are women in disguise or men in disguise, it would mean that a heterosexual marriage between a person with a homosexual disposition from neural biology and a person of the opposite sex would be illicit, because this would actually be a true gay marriage. If the gay boy married the girl, but he is actually a girl in disguise, the marriage would be illicit because they both are actually girls.

Even though such a marriage would be open to life, it is not actually a marriage because they are ultimately members of the same sex and not different sexes.

It is a little bit like saying that a person who throws away the things that came from God in the religion he followed outside the church in order to join the church could not be said to be following the Holy Spirit, because the Spirit would not tell him to reject what was true in the religion he came from, but only to reject the things that were false. The boy is rejecting what he was really made for and marrying this girl, the convert is rejecting God in order to join God's church.

The only way that a boy who was actually a girl could legitimately marry is if he retained his sex organ and married a girl who was actually a boy who retained hers.

He may desire a boy rather than a girl, but he marries this girl because she is a boy in disguise, and thus they have a legitimate marriage.

It is a bit like saying that the person outside the church who follows God ought not to throw away what was good in the religion he came from, but rather to add the mysteries of Christ's death and resurrection to what he already believed which was true and to adapt the rest of what he believed to the truths contained in the church, and thus be legitimately within the church (and part of the divine marriage). He holds onto the God he knew before, while joining God's church, and the boy is embracing what he was made for and marrying this girl. This way is the correct way to the marriage, but the former is the incorrect way.

Now, suppose that we discovered that a person's biology was able to change in such a way that a brain that was originally designed for a sexual attraction to one sex changed and it developed in such a way that it became inclined to the other sex.

If this could exist, and what I wrote above is all true, then the only way to explain that would be that the gender of the person was then changing. I am aware of magisterial statements claiming that it is not up to the person to decide his own gender, and that we must accept the gender that God gave to us. I am not aware of a magisterial statement that claims that God cannot change the gender He gives to a person.

There are many animals that in fact are able to change their genders. Clownfish, for example, are able to change their sex - a male clownfish can become a female and bear children.

With the example I gave of the Welshman above, supposing that the anecdote was completely factual, a question one would ask was whether the person was designed for males all along, and because of his environment and psychological influences, he developed an attraction for women he was not designed for prior to the stroke? Or if he was still designed for women after the stroke, and the stroke just altered his brain in some way that a new area was activated that was still actually designed for women, but somehow his new experience of it caused him to find it satisfied in men? Or if, more bizarrely, his brain originally was designed for women, and the stroke altered in such a way, that it was designed for men.

If the third possibility above was true, then it is possible for a human's sex to change, and this also does not do anything to refute the church's stance against gender ideology that puts the human being as the one who decides his own gender, rather than God. Because if the brain changes, both the new brain and the old brain were both created by God and not by human beings, and gender is therefore still from God and not from human beings. The injury or the other thing that came artificially may have caused the brain to change from one form to the other, but both forms were created by God through nature and not by people themselves. The injury killed off part of the brain, but the surviving part was not created by the injury, it rather came from nature itself and the injury allowed it to take over.

Supposing that one day human beings themselves were able to change the brain in such a way or to cause the brain to change itself in such a way, it would mean that human beings would be able to then change the sex. In that event, gender would seem to become a human choice and no longer a divine choice.

But it may be that human beings never find a way to do that. It could also be the case that while clownfish can go through such natural sex changes, that humans in fact cannot, and that what I am writing is true, but it refers to hypothetical cases only and not ones that exist in reality.

Now, suppose that the teaching about the hidden gender is true, it would however create two complications that might be difficult to grapple with, but which are not flaws that refute the entire premise.

Firstly, it would mean that there are in fact people in this world who actually do have two moms or two dads, because one of the parents was a person who was homosexual from birth.

It would also mean that there are people who were ordained to the priesthood who were not actually priests, and that there are perhaps 'women' who are not actually women who do have vocations to the priesthood, and that there are people with female vocations who were born as 'male' but not actually so.

One has to ask here whether or not such a thing is really possible. Whether we can consider that God would allow such a thing within His creation.

I have often thought that Adam must have been born from hominid parents who were not made in the image of God. If the human being derived from evolution, and this is partly what the bible means when it tells us that God made man from the dust of the Earth, then it would mean that Adam himself did not have 'human' parents when he was born, because his parents, while perhaps extremely similar to him genetically, would not have possessed the soul made in the image of God, but they would have had animal souls.

Scientific research tells us that the earliest common male ancestor of all human beings could not have been later than an estimated 300,000-200,000 years ago. If this is true, then Adam must have been either at that time or (more likely) before that time.

When Adam was born, the hominid species he was born

from most likely still existed upon the Earth. And because all human beings (ie. people made in the image of God and not just hominids) need to have Adam as their ancestor in order to be human beings, it would mean that all the hominids who did not descend from Adam would continue to have animal souls rather than souls made in the divine image. And theoretically both those hominids who descended from Adam and those who didn't would have lived next to each other at the same time.

I think it is extremely likely that these hominids who had animal souls and the descendants of Adam probably existed alongside one another for quite some time. It also seems likely that perhaps the sinful descendants of Adam after the fall could have easily interbred with these hominids who didn't descend from Adam, and maybe this forms part of the meaning when it tells us that before the flood, the Earth was filled with corruption. Bestiality is a sin, even if the animal is so similar to a human.

Would the offspring of these unions be human or animal, however?

I am not sure if I know the answer to this question other than pointing out that there is a certain probability that there are in fact people living today, maybe even all people in the world, who have ancestors that gave birth to offspring with a hominid spouse that possessed an animal soul, and that offspring was their ancestor.

If the offspring of a union of a human and an animal did not possess a human soul made in God's image, then that means that the offspring had an animal soul. If that is true, then all the descendants of that creature also would not possess a human soul, but would have an animal soul as well, even if it mated with a human. The problem is that the likelihood of mixing between the two groups, those who descended from Adam and the hominids that did not descend from Adam, is highly likely to have occurred and it may be the truth that a lot of people (perhaps all) living in the world today are actually the product of such unions. Which in turn would logically mean that if a human and a non-human's child is not human, then none of us are human either, so long as the assumption is correct that Adam's descendants had offspring with hominids that were not made in God's image.

A scientist perhaps could answer this question I will put here, because I do not know the answer. The question is: is it possible that all people in the world, given all the genetic diversity, could all have come from the gene sets of only two people who mated at the same time (ie. one who had XY chromosomes and one who had XX chromosomes), and all the genetic diversity in the world could have come from those four chromosomes with no additional genetic information at all?

I am not in a position to answer that, but if it could be

answered, and the answer is a negative, it would essentially set down the fact that there are people living today who descended from unions of humans and animals, if we continue to believe that at the beginning there were only two humans with souls made in the image of God and they came from hominid parents of a species that had animal souls.

In 2003 at a medical university in Shanghai, the world's first human-animal hybrid was created in a laboratory. It was produced with human sperm and a rabbit egg, and the embryo was able to take life and go through the beginning cell divisions. The scientists destroyed the embryo, however, before it could gain much size. This experiment has been repeated many times in other countries, with much of the public being unaware of it. If the union of a human and a hominid is a human being, then the union of a rabbit and a human must also be possessing a human soul made in God's image. What this person will look like in the resurrection, I have no idea.

But what needs to be considered here is if in fact this is possible, then that means it is in fact possible for a person to be born by parents who did not possess human souls, then why would it be impossible for a person to be born by parents who did not possess a combination of male and female souls? If a person can be born with two animal parents like Adam or with one animal parent, as is perhaps the case for many of the generations after Adam, then why should we think it is impossible for a person to be born with two mothers or two fathers?

In 2008, there was an experiment done in the United States which successfully created the first cloned human embryos, which took the DNA of a male scientist and put it into a woman's egg cell, but the cell nucleus (and the woman's chromosomes) had been removed, so that only the man's DNA was present, thus making it a clone. The embryo developed and the cells divided and grew in number, before it was destroyed.

Now, theoretically, it should be possible to do the same experiment using the woman's own DNA being placed in her egg cell and making a clone of herself. And if that is so, then even if everything else in this book is false, the fact that a person can exist without a parent from one sex will be proven true.

I am under the impression that this experiment has been claimed to have been done by others and maybe it already has been proven true that you can have a person without a male parent, but not having enough knowledge, I can't say much about it.

Adam was made from the dust and Eve was made from the rib; so it is that the male vocation is towards the entire creation and the female vocation is towards the

one thing that mattered more than the whole creation
(the person).

The girl born in the boy's body will also have a
vocation from God for persons and relationships. The
boy born in the girl's body will have a vocation from
God for work with the created world in service of
persons.

If this assumption is true and such transgendered
persons really do exist, then it would also mean that
there are men ordained to the priesthood who were not
actually ordained, because the ordination does nothing
to them and they are still incapable of performing the
sacraments, because they are not really men and they
possess female souls.

Every time they do mass, the transformation would not
occur and the bread they hand out is still just bread.
Every time they give absolution, no absolution is given,
because they never became priests in the first place. If
such men became bishops, any new priests or bishops
they ordained (assuming there was no co-celebrant)
also remain as they were before without receiving a true
ordination.

Now, is this really possible?

With regard to what I said about the hominids, I think it

is likely although I don't know for sure. But with this scenario, I will state 100% that it is completely possible, because this scenario can exist whether or not the things I wrote about the possibility of the hidden gender are true.

In fact it already did happen in a way, because when the Church of England broke with the Pope, eventually they lost the validity of their sacraments because they failed to maintain the proper ordination, and even if some of them in later times believes the Catholic interpretation of the sacraments, these sacraments were still not true sacraments.

But can it happen in the church united with Peter?

Let us suppose that in the 11th century somewhere in a rural part of Germany with no parish priest there was a little boy that was baptized by his grandmother. The grandmother takes the boy and pours water on his head, saying, 'I baptize you in the name of Jesus Christ the Saviour!'

What's the problem?

The Catholic Church teaches that this is an invalid baptism. The child needs to be baptized with the Trinitarian formula (ie. Father, Son and Holy Spirit), otherwise the baptism is invalid and the child needs to get baptized again.

However, this child doesn't know what happened because he was too young to understand and he grows up and forgets about it. He is an unbaptized person his whole life, but he doesn't know that he is unbaptized. And he continues life until death in this state while regularly taking the sacraments within the church from the priest who believes him to be a baptized catholic, which he also believes himself to be. (I think anyone who insists that the unbaptized cannot be saved should seriously consider this possibility)

When he gets older, he joins a monastery and is ordained to the priesthood. However, the ordination to the priesthood did not actually occur, since the sacrament of Holy Orders cannot be given to someone who wasn't baptized. The church teaches that to receive the sacrament you must be a baptized male; if you are not a male, you cannot receive the sacrament, and if you are not baptized, you cannot receive it either.

Therefore, he remains as an unbaptized person and when he does mass the transformation of the Eucharist does not occur, but it is only just bread and wine in his hands that he gives out to the faithful. This man then gets ordained to be a bishop of the area. He ordains men to the priesthood, but every person he ordains remains just as a lay catholic, since he was incapable of giving this sacrament because he was never a bishop, never a priest and never actually baptized.

But the priests he ordains themselves do not know this

and they give the sacraments to others as well, but no one realizes that these are not actually true sacraments because these men never actually became priests. This bishop himself ordains other men to be bishops, but these people also do not become bishops either.

However, because they think they are bishops, they then ordain other priests and other bishops after them, and thus you form a big web of people going down for many years, even centuries, wherein all these people remained as laity and every sacrament they gave was invalid (except for baptism, which can be done by anyone, even by an unbaptized person).

What I wrote about hidden gender persons does not at all need to be true in order for this scenario to have ever existed or to exist now. Hence, I write that it is 100% possible for such a thing to exist. Whether or not it has ever happened, I do not know.

In the modern day, the church accepts baptisms done legitimately in other denominations for people entering the church after an investigation is done. However, it is certainly possible that some human mistake, neglect to do appropriate checks or an error in judgment could be made in the course of this investigation and a person who received an invalid baptism in another denomination is admitted to the sacraments through the RCIA. If such a person ever became a priest or bishop, this scenario I write above would then be a reality. The hidden gender does not need to exist in order for this to be possible in the church, in the past or now.

There are many gay clergy within the church, but that doesn't mean that they all have a hidden gender, even if the hidden gender exists – they could be psychological homosexuals. However, if what I write is true, then any priest or bishop who was possessing of a sexual attraction to a man, which came from biology and not from psychology, would be unable to give any sacraments except baptism, since they were never ordained in the first place. It would be incredibly scandalous and damaging to the church if this were publicly revealed… but being scandalous and damaging does nothing to refute it as being a real possibility, and in fact such a scenario is entirely possible, as I mentioned, without anything I write about the hidden gender being true, since an unbaptized bishop would necessarily mean the same thing for the church.

It would be unwise to assume it couldn't exist, just because such a thing would seem to hurt the church so much.

Catholics have much guilt in the question of religious indifference and being the source that causes people of other religions to think that their religions are true. Is it possible that God could punish the church like this for that sin: that He allowed them to be deceived and receive sacraments that were not truly sacraments, letting them be deceived that what they were receiving was true? Just as they failed to inform those in other faiths about what the Truth was, therefore God left them in the deception that they were receiving the sacraments of the church from their priest who was not actually a priest?

What I say about a person being born gay does not at all need to be true, for this to have ever happened. Everything in this book can be false... and this will still be a possibility.

The church is a body, and bodies have immune systems that combat viruses and unwanted intruders, even without the person being aware of what the body is doing. When priests co-celebrate a mass and they say the words of consecration together, I think it only needs to be the case that one of those priests saying the words needs to be a genuine priest and the consecration occurs. The church has long held the practice of using multiple bishops as co-celebrants for ordaining bishops and sometimes even priests. Usually each bishop performs the laying on of hands, but only one bishop does the anointing with oil. If the bishops laid their hands, but someone else anointed with the oil, would the sacrament still be given? I am not sure, but if it is, then it is also true that in an ordination, you only needed one of the bishops to be valid and the whole sacrament would then be valid. It could be like the immune system of the body, in that the church already has mechanisms built into its traditions that can root out such a thing from spreading if it ever happened.

In 2005 Benedict XVI banned all people with homosexual desires from ordination to the priesthood, and required that they had to be free of the attraction for at least three years beforehand. Pope Francis reaffirmed this ban as well. It was not for the reasons I laid out in this book, but this ban is solving this problem, if in fact this problem is real. It is also perhaps the body's immune system at work.

Even if they rise up to be a Vatican Cardinal, they are still only a layperson and do not possess any of the spiritual powers given by the Holy Spirit to those ordained with Holy orders.

Keep in mind, a person does not need to be a priest in order for the Holy Spirit to work in him. He does not need to be ordained to the priesthood to act as an instrument to save the souls of people and bring them to God. Even should a person have followed his life, thinking he was a priest and he wasn't, this does not at all mean he did nothing good and his work was not of merit, nor does it mean that Christ and His Spirit did not do good works through him.

Similarly, this could also mean that there are some

people born as women, who are actually males due to the sexual orientation within their neural biology, but who may in fact have a vocation to the priesthood, episcopate or permanent diaconate. And if they were ordained they could in fact do the sacraments and the sacraments would be licit; their bread and wine would become the Body and Blood, their absolutions would absolve the sins of the penitent, etc. Woman priests actually could be possible, if this is all true, but they just wouldn't really be women.

If the gender of the person was able to change, it would have interesting connotations to the question of ordination as well. Since the sacrament can only be given to a person once, but it cannot be given to a female, then I would speculate (although I don't know for sure) that a male who received it and became a female as a result of some biological change in the brain that altered his sexuality, would always have the ordination remaining on him/her, but would no longer be capable of performing sacraments if he became a she, because it has to be done by a baptized male, since the priest is in the place of the bridegroom. But if the neural sex reversed back again, then perhaps the ordination would not need to be repeated in order for the sacraments to be valid.

It is similar to saying that if a bishop had his hands cut off in some accident, he could not validly give ordination to someone else, because the ordination requires him to place his hands on the person's head, otherwise the sacrament is not given. As long as the hands were missing, it would be impossible for him to do this sacrament.

If it was possible to actually alter the sex of a person, then I think all sacraments (except for baptism) the person performed would be invalid so long as the sex was female. It would have to turn back into a male again in order for the sacraments to be valid.

I question whether it is possible to alter the sex, for reasons that I will get into later, but just speaking as a possibility, I think that this would be how it worked hypothetically.

There are many homosexuals who are very creative and very intelligent people. Perhaps it is just my imagination, but I am not the only person who has thought this either. Even when God gives burdens to people, He gives them gifts as well. And these gifts can be used for great purposes.

Leonardo da Vinci never had a wife and he is sometimes thought to have been homosexual on the basis of him being held up for charges of sodomy on one occasion, but was acquitted because one of the others with him who here held up on the same charge had connections with a powerful family. We are perhaps never going to know really.

Michelangelo, the famous Italian painter who did many of the great works that are on the ceilings and walls of the Vatican, has often been thought to have perhaps been a homosexual person.

He (and Leonardo too) was like a modern-day Bezalel. Bezalel could work with stone, wood and do all sorts of different kinds of artistic work that was needed to produce the holy items used by the Jewish people that were listed in Exodus. These two men were talented in so many ways, and a lot of their talents were used for the creation of holy artwork for use in churches.

Some have suggested that Antoni Gaudi, the designer of the Sagrada Familia in Barcelona, may have been bisexual as well... but I do not really know very much about this.

In recent years some people have even suggested that Leonardo's mysterious painting, the Mona Lisa, is actually a portrait of himself as a woman. There is only one known portrait of Leonardo that was made in his lifetime （done by himself） when he was an old man, and some have suggested that his facial features have a similarity to the Mona Lisa. It could also be complete coincidence, however. The more traditional narrative about the Mona Lisa was that Leonardo was attempting to do a portrait for a particular noblewoman. Although both of these explanations could have been true at the same time as well.

Among Michelangelo's many pieces of art that would decorate the Vatican, one of his most famous is the very large painting he did of the Final Judgement of Christ.

Since the 17th century, the room that houses this painting (the Sistine chapel) has also been the place where all papal elections were held. It is interesting to know that the cardinals who chose the Pope do it under a portrait reminding them of the punishment due upon sinners at Christ's return. I suppose it is a reminder that they better make sure that they choose according to their conscience.

Michelangelo was well criticized in his own time for making all this nude art in a holy place like the Vatican.

In the painting, at the bottom right, there is an image of hell. The lord of hell, Minos, is standing with a snake around his body and a snake biting his genitals.

This part of the painting has a story behind it. Michelangelo's critics complained that it was so scandalous that all these nude figures could be painted on the walls of the Vatican. One of Michelangelo's critics was the Papal Master of Ceremonies Biagio da Cesena.

The story goes that when Biagio da Cesena harshly criticized Michelangelo while he was drawing this painting, Michelangelo drew Biagio into the painting as 'Minos' the lord of hell with a snake biting his genitals and thus keeping them covered. When Biagio went to the Pope to complain about this, the Pope seemed to like the joke, and he replied that he had no jurisdiction over hell and thus could not change it for him.

It is a good reminder in a place like that, where the cardinals elect the pope, that not all the bishops and cardinals are going to inherit salvation, and they must follow what they know is True and act according to their conscience or else they could end up as lords of hell rather than servants in heaven.

Every piece of art on Earth, has an interpretation in heaven, even an interpretation that the author was not thinking of.

I want to write here an interpretation I have of one of the mysteries of the final tribulation. It may be right or wrong, I cannot guarantee, but it is worth sharing in reference to all of this.

The beast that comes from the land and the beast that comes from the sea in Revelations; they may also be Behemoth and Leviathan in Job. The beast on the land causes the people to worship the beast from the sea; Behemoth brings the world to worship Leviathan.

Leviathan rules them and conquers them.

What are these two?

Athanasius said to the pagans that they ought to worship the person who crafted the idol rather than the idol itself because the creator is greater than the creation. And of course, then in turn, the person who created the person who created the idol must be even more worthy of worship.

The human being is the greatest thing that was created and if one could ever worship a created thing, this would be the one thing that mattered more than anything else.

Among all human beings, who were the greatest that God created?

Was it Kings, Emperors, poets, conquerors, philosophers?

One could argue that the Virgin Mary had the greatest role among all humans that God created (Christ Himself was not created). If one worshipped her as a god in place of her Son, it would be the greatest thing that could be made into an idol.

In my book *Witchcraft* I imagined that there is a female vocation shared by Mary and other women that I called a wei'nu, which is perhaps the greatest kind of role given to created human beings, although I could be wrong about whether or not it truly exists.

Apart from that, however, there is no role for human beings greater than the ordained priesthood. Of all the things that God created, the greatest was the human being, and among all the roles that human beings fulfill, the greatest is the priesthood.

So, of all the created things that one can make into an idol, here is the ultimate idol. Instead of worshipping God and His Son, we worship the priests He created instead.

It is turning the priests into an idol and it is turning the church into a kind of idol, because people are thinking that the church has a power to change the gospel given from the Father through the Son, which is a power that Christ Himself didn't have. Turning the church into an idol is a bit like turning the Virgin Mary into an idol, since the church is intimately connected with her. Putting the church on a higher footing than Christ and His gospel is a bit like putting the Virgin Mary in front of God.

And in truth, the church has long already had the smoke of this idolatry in the church since ancient times. Whenever people believed that the bishops or the priests had the right to change the church's teachings, they were already following an idol and no longer following God, because the bishops were created too.

I don't simply mean modern thinking at all by this. Go

back into the history of the church and observe the times when people thought that unjust war was acceptable if the bishop or priest approved, that rebellion was acceptable if the bishop or priest approved, that unfair treatment of the poor was acceptable if the bishop or priest approved, that unfair treatment of religious minorities was acceptable if the bishop or priest approved, that slavery which reduced the human being to a commodity was acceptable if the bishop or priest approved, … people at that time were already following an idol, because the bishop had no power to change the law of God. To place anything in front of God is an act of idolatry, and the faithful Catholic who believes the bishop has the power to approve violations of God’s law is following the bishop, a created thing, and not following God. It is an idol.

Cardinal Marx of Germany said it perfectly at the Synod of the family in October 2015, ‘We don’t own the Truth; the Truth owns us.’

If the bishops are the ones who decide what the Truth is, then we are following an idol. It is because I follow the Truth and not the opinions of people that I am able to write this book.

But I think it is not just the clergy, but there will be

something else as well. Augustine of Hippo, in his last chapter of his famous book 'The Confessions', wrote an interpretation of the first chapter of Genesis and gave symbolic meanings to every part of the narrative. He thought that the land represented the church and the sea represented outside of the church. Perhaps the first beast (Leviathan) is from outside the church and the second beast (Behemoth) is from inside the church.

I think that perhaps Behemoth is an individual priest or bishop, although maybe it refers to many priests or bishops; he is the beast on the land that makes the world worship the beast from the sea, Leviathan, who is perhaps the secular ruler, like the Roman Emperor in the time of the early church.

The secular authority is not greater than the priestly authority, but true perversion is the submission of the latter to the former. Both are idols, because they are placed in front of God, but the secular authority is the one that is openly worshipped.

It is said that the number 666 (which was the number of the first beast that the second beast required all to put on their foreheads and hands), was a number that stood for the name of 'Nero Caesar', since his name in Hebrew characters had the numeric value of 666. Nero also killed himself with a neck wound. The beast in revelations is described as having a head that was mortally wounded.

The first beast will be someone like Nero, perhaps. Just

as John the Baptist was Elijah, so also the antichrist will be Nero. Not the same person, but a person like him, in the same spirit and role. An insane earthly-ruler who lives a terribly sinful life, who seeks to destroy the church and bring the world to worship him as a god.

The beast on the land has the semblance of a lamb, but speaks like a dragon- like a clergyman who seems holy and yet fools people into following something false.

The harlot seated on top of the seven hills, and the false prophet and Behemoth, could be interpreted as referring to the same person or persons (it can of course have more than one correct interpretation as well)- it is perhaps like a bishop of Rome who is unfaithful to God, and who deceives the world into worshipping the first beast to whom the dragon gives his throne. Harlotry in the bible is often a symbol for idolatry.

Jesus promised Peter that the gates of hell would never prevail against him. He didn't make this same promise to the other apostles. Hence, the Pope's authority can always be trusted or else Christ's words are untrue. But suppose someone attains the office unlawfully, and the legitimate Pope, who openly does not recognize the false pope, is unable to rule the church, because he is under persecution. Then in this case, you can have a bishop of Rome (who is not truly the bishop of Rome) who will deceive the church and whose authority cannot be trusted. And all the bishops and clergy who join with him and break communion with the true pope, will also lose their legitimate authority as well, because they essentially form a schismatic church and not the true church founded by Christ upon Peter.

Peter, and those in communion with him, can always be trusted in their authority, from now all the way until the second coming. But if bishops break themselves from this rock, then the gates of hell can overcome them and they can deceive the world.

There are three prominent cities in the world that were built on seven hells: Rome, Istanbul and Moscow. The latter two are important centres of Eastern Orthodoxy. At one time, Istanbul was also the seat of the Sunni Caliphate. The harlot that sits on the seven hills can also be referring to the church and body of believers that is following the false prophet that speaks from the authority of those hills, and they will persecute the people who hold fast to the Truth. I suppose if Orthodoxy ever took control of the city of Rome and made a false bishop of Rome to direct the world to worship Leviathan, it would be a way in which this could be carried out. Different sources have sometimes interpreted Magog to be referring to various peoples like Scythians, Huns or Mongols that lived in or invaded from territories associated with modern Russia.

If you can even imagine it at that time what it could be like; intense persecution of those who follow the truth, and incredible suffering like Job, while the people praising the persecution are the leaders of the church themselves, but not those who legitimately hold such authority because they are not in communion with the true Pope, and who preach that they have the authority to change the church's teachings, and they tell the people to worship Leviathan as a god, who also rules them.

And thus, the church from its beginning days when it endured persecution in order to avoid worshipping the Emperor, then comes full circle and the clergy demand of the faithful to worship this ruler or rulers, from outside of the church, as their god, and those who fail to do so are treated with incredible persecution, as though they were enemies of God condemned to hell.

This spirit is already in the world, however. Every time the faithful follow the sinful ways of the world rather than God's law, because they think that the priest or bishop gives them approval, they are already following this idol.

I wonder if perhaps also the beasts could also be like an evil parallel to Christ and Mary. In that one is male and the other is female, or one gives birth to the other, or one is a priest and the other is a woman that had the vocation of a wei'nu (see my book *Witchcraft*). Behemoth, the priest, makes the world turn to worship Leviathan, the wei'nu, as their true ruler in the place of the living God. That is supposing that wei'nu exist, and if they don't, then Leviathan may be someone different, but still an earthly ruler.

Of all that God made, nothing was greater than the human being. And of all the roles He gave to the human being, nothing was greater than this.

There is no idol greater than this one. There is no created thing that one can worship that will surpass these. There is nothing else to be added to the deception and temptation after that point; it will be finished.

And thus the two beasts, the one from the sea and the one from the land, Behemoth and Leviathan, both created by God and left to astound the suffering Job or the persecuted church in the final suffering who stays true to the faith at the time of the antichrist, and ultimately serving to point out to Job and the church of the final persecution how great God's glory was that He could make even these.

Lord, we pray that you help us to understand the things that are possible and impossible in relation to homosexuality and these things discussed here. We pray for the church to receive wisdom about how best to deal with these issues and not to be led into deception.

We ask for these things, if it is your will, in Jesus'
name, Amen

IX: Hidden Spiritual Realities

Nothing in this world happens by coincidence. Every
dot, every detail, every thing that happens, all occurs for
a reason, although the reason is often hidden to us
human beings.

In the bible, you can read the chronicles of the kings of
Israel and learn history not just from a presentation of
facts but also to see the hidden spiritual realities that
were occurring in the nation's history and how God was
involved in the nation. The invasion of a foreign power
was not just because of historical circumstances, but it
was because of the sin of the people for generations of
idolatry that had caused it.

I have already written that I believe there is a profound
connection between the mystery of people seeking
salvation outside the church and the mystery of
homosexuality. There are some things I want to add to
what I have already written that I will include here.

Firstly, I believe that if homosexuality is biological, then it may be the case that even if Adam and Eve had never eaten the fruit, there still may have been people born as biological homosexuals. Just as Jesus told the disciples that the man born blind was not from his parents' sin, so also the biological homosexual was not from his parents, up to and including Adam and Eve. In that case, God in fact did design people to be this way.

However, the belief in ancestral sin causing misfortune to later descendants is commonly found in the bible. Moses says that your sins will be brought upon your descendants to the third and fourth generation. David's son dies in infancy because of David's own sin. God tells Eli that for the sins of his sons, the future generations of his family will be punished for it. God says about Solomon that the kingdom will be taken away from his son because of Solomon's sins. And the most obvious case of all, of course, is the fact that death and suffering enter the world because of one man's sin that is visited upon all of his descendants.

I believe that ancestral sin is a spiritual reality, not just with Adam and Eve, but for all people. It means that people in their lives can experience consequences that are falling on them due to the sins committed by their ancestors before them.

The sins that we commit are visited upon our descendants and we inherit things that resulted from the sins of our near ancestors. It is not only the case the man who commits sin will cause his children to be born in worse conditions, like as though his gambling lost the inheritance, or something directly attributable through rational causes like that, but it is actually the case that people are going to mysteriously suffer things in life simply because their parents, grand-parents and great-grandparents had done things that are going to be visited upon them.

This should not be understood as a punishment upon the individuals themselves, because how can you be punished for a crime that you don't commit?

Original sin is not the personal sin of us, nor is it the punishment of us, but we have to suffer its effects because of the punishment upon Adam and Eve for committing it.

The way that ancestral sin perhaps ought to be understood is that people receive graces from God, which they are able to pass on their descendants after them, but those graces can be denied to the descendants if the ancestors committed a sin that offended God. Adam and Eve inherited paradise and they had the ability to pass it on to their descendants, but for their sin, they were cast out from it and lost the ability to pass it on and thus all people had to suffer the consequences. It is not that God was punishing future generations for what Adam and Eve did, but it is rather that God gave a gift to Adam and Eve, which they would have been able to pass on had it not been for their own failing.

The same is true in other instances. God gave the kingdom to Solomon or the priesthood to Eli, and either one had the ability to pass it on if only they had not sinned. David inherited life from God and he could have given it to his son, had it not been for his own sin.

It is not a punishment to the descendant, it is a punishment for the ancestor that is visited upon the descendant. The punishment is only on the individual who commits the act, but the consequences extend further than the punishment and I believe that they can in fact be transmitted through generations in a mysterious way. Not just for original sin, but for all sins. I could be wrong in my understanding.

I should clarify something: I don't mean to say that everything that people suffer in life is because of the sins of their own ancestors. What I mean is that there may be things in life that they suffer because of those sins, but there might also be things that they suffer that have no relation to those sins.

Christ took on suffering for the sins of the whole world, including those who were His earthly ancestors and those who were not His earthly ancestors. All suffering is coming from sin, but people can suffer many things that come from neither their own sins or the sins of their ancestors, but from the sins of other people.

Nor is it true that a particular sin will always have the same punishment when done by different people in different instances. Hence, even if God punishes people for doing something in one way, that doesn't mean that He will always punish other people with the same punishment when they commit the same crime.

If I am correct in what I think, however, then I think that LGBT things may also be sometimes connected with sins of ancestors. That is to say, that the things that are being suffered by LGBT persons in their lives may in fact sometimes be mysteriously connected to sins that were committed by their parents, grandparents or great-grandparents before them, just as Moses said that sins will be visited on descendants to the third and fourth generation.

In cases where the person has a homosexual attraction from psychology and not from biology, it may even be true that one could say that this person is gay because of sins committed by their ancestors. In cases where the person has a homosexual attraction from biology and not from psychology, the person would have been gay even if Adam and Eve themselves didn't sin, but the person might still suffer things in their lives, which are in fact related to sins that occurred in the generations before them.

The same is true of transgendered persons. There may be people who are transgendered because their ancestors before them committed sins that made them such. There may also be people born with a hidden gender that would have had the hidden gender regardless of anyone's sins, but who might still suffer things in life because of what their ancestors did.

What I speculate about regarding this in particular is whether ancestral sin in this instance could have anything to do with sins that people commit in failing to follow God's plan for the spiritual marriage between the Bridegroom and the Bride.

What I mean is that the spiritual marriage in heaven is that God is going to marry His church, and thus He calls all people to believe the gospel, receive baptism and to spread the good news to others. Many people resist this call, and I wonder if it is possible that the resistance to this call could in fact be causing them to lose certain graces that are then lost to their next generations who become gay or transgendered, or who suffer things as people who have a hidden gender, as a result.

Not in all instances, of course, but some people who

suffer or possess these things might have this relation with what their ancestors did. Nor would it necessarily be the case that every person who commits this sin would receive this kind of misfortune upon their descendants as opposed to something different. However, in some instances, this may be true.

For example, suppose that a family lives in a Catholic country, and the gospel is easily accessible to them – it is not the case that they are being kept away from it by circumstances beyond their control. However, they have such deep distrust for the church that they refuse to listen to it or believe its teachings, and thus they spiritually try to find happiness in the created world without seeking salvation inside the church founded by the Creator. In this way, the Bride tries to marry the Bride, rather than to seek the spiritual marriage with the Bridegroom, and this spiritual sin then causes the family to produce children who desire to have relations with people of the same sex (in the case of psychological homosexuality) or it causes the family's children that would have been gay regardless of sin (in the case of biological homosexuality) but who nevertheless suffer all sorts of things in life in relation to their orientation.

This is speculative on my part, and obviously it could be wrong. Or alternatively it could also be right, but simply far more complicated and deeper than I am theorizing here.

People who distrust the Truth and the church and see it
as a force for evil, and thus refuse to listen to it; the
distrust perhaps goes on for generation after
generation. It is like a woman who is born heterosexual,
but because of psychology, she is unable to feel a trust
for men, and develops a sexual desire for women. I
speculate that people who develop such things in life
might actually have some kind of connection with these
sorts of sins committed prior to them.

People who love the world so much and see the church
and its teachings as an obstacle to their own happiness,
so that they refuse to convert to it, perhaps going on for
generations. A child is produced to them that finds the
homosexual relationship so much more enjoyable than
the heterosexual one. What he experiences, in seeing
the unnatural relation so much more pleasing than the
natural one, is just like the people who find marrying
this world so much more pleasing than marrying God.

Within the church founded by Christ the idea exists
quite strongly that encourages people in thinking like it
is not right to try to convert others to the church, like
we need to respect other religions so much that we
should never try to get them to believe the true religion

or that there is just ultimately no need to try to get other people to believe in our faith. This is something that the church defines as the sin of 'indifference' and it is a great temptation in our modern day for Catholics, including the clergy themselves, to fall into this sin and come to think that we no longer have any need to try to bring the faith to others.

If Christ truly is not actually concerned about whether or not people believe Him or His church, this is almost the same thing as though the Bridegroom no longer desires women.

People commit this sin and perhaps a consequence for it is that children develop homosexual or transgender tendencies, or they are born with a natural hidden gender and must suffer things as a result of their parents' decisions that lost graces by their sins.

The people in nations that try to build utopias through human efforts alone and without the need for religion. In some states, they try to reject religion and the reliance on any kind of heavenly help, and seek to create a prosperous society without the presence of religion. It is like the bride rejects men and is trying to marry the bride.

I had an experience once, when I was in a park in Beijing near Chongwenmen and some men approached me to talk to me, since they were curious in me as a foreigner. They told me that they were homosexuals and I had a conversation with them. An image in my head that I still remember is seeing them standing under a huge statue in the park depicting communist soldiers and/or workers (can't clearly remember) standing heroically in some pose. I remember thinking to myself at the time that these two images were connected.

The generations of people that sought to make a new world without religion where all problems would be solved, and in the end the homosexuality or sufferings related to it come about as a result. Not in all instances, but with some, perhaps it is truly like this.

People who have such discomfort over the Truth that they and all people must enter the church for salvation. They want this reality to change so that this is no longer true. It is like people who can't stand the reality of their own gender.

The creator of the transgender TV series *Transparent* is a Jewish woman with a father who transitioned to become a woman and the series itself heavily centred on Jewish issues. I don't know what it is statistically, but it often seems to me like there is a significantly large number of Jews that are either gay or transgender, as a proportion of the total LGBT population in relation to what Jews actually are in proportion to the general population. Perhaps that is just my imagination, however, and not a statistical reality.

If it is not my imagination, however, then it is worth considering whether the obstinacy of so many generations of Jews living in Christian countries that refused to believe the Messiah that was preached to them could in fact cause such a result among their descendants.

I have heard statistics, however, about huge number of young males in Thailand that identify as transgendered, far more than in other parts of the world.

Thailand, of course, is a deeply Buddhist country. In Thailand, people can be very offended if you went there to try to convert them to Christianity. The call for people to convert to the gospel of the True God is a shameful call to make. The wrongness of the Bridegroom's call for conversion; the discomfort of being a man – perhaps there is a connection here.

People find it so shameful for Christians to come and tell them to convert to Christ. Perhaps the punishment for the people who think that such a thing is shameful and thus reject the divine marriage is for their descendants to suffer things related to this and reject their own gender identity.

Again, I am speculating here, and I could easily be wrong. Or the reality could also be more complex and deeper than the understanding I am presenting here.

Moses said that the sins of people are visited to their descendants to the third and fourth generation.

In the 21st century we are currently living in a unique time period in the world's history. There are fewer and fewer spots in the world where it can truly be said any longer that the reason why people lack knowledge of the gospel is because it was impossible for people in that place to have had an opportunity to hear it. Globalization, technology, the internet and all sorts of other factors have made it such that the opportunity to hear these things has spread to almost all corners of the world.

However, most of the world still does not believe it. In some cases, this is an innocent unawareness, but in others it is a sinful rejection and also in some cases it is a sinful indifference that refuses to preach it.

Whereas those places before may have been innocent, because they never had the opportunity to hear the gospel and commit the sin, once the gospel is spread there and they still don't listen to it, their innocence is lost. It may be the case that the spread of the gospel in modern times, as well as the growing rejection and indifference to the mission of its spread, may also be related to the LGBT things that grow stronger and more widespread in the modern-day.

Political states changed to give full toleration to every religious belief without trying to pressure anyone to conversion. This was considered something enlightened and modern. In just the same way, the same political machinery employs the same arguments, the same feelings, the same justifications, and proclaims rights to LGBT people.

In just the same way as the society changed to say that every religious belief is acceptable and became fully indifferent to the missionary call, so also does the society come to fully embrace LGBT things, to teach it to children and have it represented well in the media.

In the same way that people abandon the call for people to believe in Christ and become accustomed or accepting to whatever people wish to believe in, so also does the society work the same way to become accustomed and accepting to whatever sexual relationship or gender that the people wish to pursue.

God's meaning is always behind all of these things. Whether or not I am correct in my interpretation of His meaning, I am uncertain.

However, although I have doubts about my

speculations, at the same time I don't think this is entirely my own imagination to think like this either, because I remember what the biblical text itself says.

Paul himself said that it was the idolatry of the Romans that led their women to exchange natural relations for unnatural ones and for the men to burn in lost for other men. The spiritual sins that they committed in exchanging the Creator for the created were related to the fact that their men and women exchanged natural relations for unnatural ones. This is what Paul said of the great city of Rome in the 1st century, which is also called Babylon. Our own great and advanced society in the 21st century is perhaps something quite similar.

As I wrote before, I don't think it is a coincidence that the entire gay rights movement in modern times and the increase in people who identify as LGBT occurred after the 1960s when the church strongly put forward ideas that people outside the church could find salvation and many Catholics stopped thinking that there was a need to convert the world any longer. I also think that this whole thing may in fact be a way in which God is going to chastise His church to get it to return to the right path.

Lord, we pray that you help us to understand the deeper spiritual realities as they apply to this issue. We pray for the whole world to hear the call of the gospel and convert to the Lord Jesus Christ who sent His apostles to establish the church and baptize all nations. We ask for these things, if it is your will, in Jesus' name, Amen

IX: Gay Conversion Therapy

This topic, I will also need to mention here.

This is a very controversial topic, and some developed countries have even put down legislation attempting to ban its existence.

In principle, at least on paper, there really should be nothing wrong with this therapy existing, so long as the people who join it or doing so willingly and not under compulsion from others.

If the first possibility (regarding the psychological origin of homosexuality) is correct, then you don't need to worry that this therapy is teaching people to reject themselves, because the heterosexual desires are their true selves and thus, they are helping people to become their true selves.

If the fourth possibility is correct, then this therapy simply needs to keep in mind that not every person is supposed to be straight, and they should try to change only those with a psychological attraction and not a biological attraction. As I stated before, I suspect the fourth possibility is the actual reality.

If the third possibility is correct, then the therapy must be completely rejected because it means that every person who experiences homosexual feelings was designed that way.

Now, that is just on paper or in principle. In reality, there are a number of problems.

Firstly, a lot of these therapies may use some kind of sexual stimulation and encourage the person to develop sexual feelings for the opposite sex.

Even though they are attempting to help the person psychologically, this has to be condemned as a form of sexual activity that is occurring outside of a marriage. Masturbation is still masturbation, no matter what circumstances it is occurring under, and thus any kind of psychological or medical treatment that employs masturbation as a tool cannot be permissible under church teaching.

Teresa of Avila said that the devil is like a noiseless file, because his temptations wear away at the virtues of people without them even being cognizant of it.

This is a reality, which one can see all the time within

the church. There are so many countless examples within the church when people do something which is objectively opposed to catholic teaching, and yet they somehow convince themselves that what they are doing is God's will. I will give some later on down below, of what I mean.

It is all part of the same idolatry that fills most of the world, even among believers, because the number of people who genuinely follow the Truth and not simply the currents of opinion or the words of human beings, I think is really quite small- whether we are speaking of those outside the church or even those within the church.

How can it possibly be that Christian voices condemn masturbation as an objective evil and yet applaud this therapy when it uses masturbation as a tool for 'conversion'?

If you think that human beings have the authority to decide when masturbation is right and when it is wrong, then you are following an idol and you are no longer following God.

If such therapy is used, then it cannot employ any sexual element at all, whether it be masturbation, whether it be pictures, whether it be even just talking about sexual things that can cause arousal... unless the person is doing it with their spouse only and in a way that is open to new life.

Secondly, there are a number of doubts that have been raised as to whether this therapy actually works or whether it damages people instead of helping them.

I can't comment on this, because I have little expertise on it. Obviously if it is psychologically harmful to people, then it probably shouldn't be allowed to exist.

Thirdly... and this point may be harder to understand... such therapy can't tell the person to reject the sexual feelings they have already.

Even if the person is a person born straight who became gay as a result of environment rather than biology, you still must not tell the person to reject their sexual feelings. Even if they are very uncomfortable with these feelings and they would be happy to reject them, it is still not correct.

Why is that?

It goes back to what the Popes wrote about human ecology and what the catechism says about accepting one's own sexual identity.

If a person born straight, has a same-sex attraction as a result of environment, this attraction he has for other males is actually an attraction for females, but it just doesn't seem like it. The way he feels about men, is the way he was designed to feel about women. The way she feels about women, is the way she was designed to feel about men.

Rather than rejecting these attractions, instead they should embrace them, and believe that these feelings they have are actually for the opposite sex, but it just doesn't seem like it.

By embracing them, I don't mean to masturbate or engage in any kind of sexual activity. I mean rather, that they must accept that these feelings are part of them rather than fight against them, and simply understand that these feelings are designed to be satisfied by the opposite sex and they are not wrong at all. They must embrace them so deeply that they recognize these things they lust after are nowhere near enough to satisfy them, they must look to heaven to give them what they want, to fulfill their wildest cravings within the ecstasy of the divine love, each according to the gender and sexual identity he was given in life.

Everything that they feel with the same sex, they are feeling it for the opposite sex! This is the logic that people perhaps do not understand. They never were gay.

They must not reject anything they feel, but must embrace it completely as part of themselves, and understand that what they fantasize about is actually the opposite sex and not the same sex, even if they can't imagine the opposite sex in that way. The boy he is thinking of and fantasizing about, this person in his mind is a girl and not a boy, but he is just confused and doesn't realize it is a girl. He is seeking after a girl, and that is why no boy is able to satisfy him, because the boy is not like the girl he fantasizes about who looks to him like a boy. He doesn't need to change his feelings, he needs to change his understanding of his feelings.

The girl she fantasizes about is a boy, not a girl, it is just that she is confused and doesn't realize that this is a boy. She was never actually gay, she was merely just confused, because the boy she desired looked like a girl in her mind's eye.

Of course, if the third or fourth possibility are true, then there will be boys who will fantasize about boys that truly are boys and some girls will fantasize about girls that truly are girls. But in reality, this is still a heterosexual attraction, because the boy fantasizing about the boy is not actually a boy and the girl fantasizing about the girl is not actually a girl.

There is actually no such true thing as a homosexual attraction in this world. All people who experience sexual attraction for the same sex are either actually desiring the opposite sex that is disguised as the same sex in their mind's eye, and they don't realize it, or they themselves are the opposite sex in disguise.

The conversion therapy must not tell people to reject
their feelings, but rather to see if it is possible that they
can enjoy the same feelings and passions within a
martial relationship with the opposite sex. But again,
the methods they employ must not use anything sexual,
unless it is in the context of a marriage open to life.

It is similar to how it is that when a person converts
from some created religion and becomes a Catholic,
regarding the way that he followed the created religion
and lived his life before- he must not reject this, but
instead he ought to take these same practices and
devotions, and apply it to the true God within the
church. Telling him to reject everything he knew before
is not a good way to convert.

You don' t use violence or warfare to convert people,
as happened in times past, unless the warfare is being
fought in a necessary defence of life. Similarly, you
don' t use masturbation or anything sexual to convert
gay orientations, unless the sexual experience is being
done within a marriage that is open to life.

All people are designed for God, which means that they
will have a natural desire for catechesis. You don' t
need to force it out of them or put it in there for them,
it is in there and it will come out on its own.

Similarly, all people are designed to be heterosexual.

You don't need to force them to be heterosexual, because they will naturally go towards it on their own.

But some people will die without ever receiving the Catholic faith, and yet still get to heaven. Some people will have been born with homosexual desires, but it will be heterosexual in disguise.

But this is only a possibility and not a certainty. I mean that for both statements, not simply the latter.

If you read the church documents carefully, you will know that the church has never in fact said that people outside the church have ever actually gone to heaven. It merely has said that they can, if certain conditions were met – but says nothing about whether there ever was or ever will be a person who meets those conditions.

The Catechism only states that if a person outside the church seeks the truth and does the will of God as he understands it, then he can be saved. But whether or not there ever was such a person in the history of the world, the church has not stated. The catechism only says that if such a person does exist, then he can be saved.

The logic of the Sacred Heart demands that this must be true, for how could God condemn those who sought after Him and yet failed to know His name through no fault of their own?

Similarly, I say that if a person has a homosexual attraction because the brain itself is designed this way, then he is the opposite sex in disguise and his attraction is a heterosexual one. But whether or not such a thing has ever existed or will ever exist- I cannot say. I am only saying that if such conditions are met, then the person is the opposite sex in disguise.

The logic of church doctrine demands that this must be this way, because otherwise it would be a contradiction with the teaching that we must accept our bodies that God made for us.

As I've already made clear before, I suspect that such people outside the church who have found salvation really have existed and do exist. Although the church itself has never explicitly stated so in its official teaching.

The closest example of such that I could think of where the church may have said someone outside the church went to heaven was in the church's celebration of the Holy Innocents (feast day Dec. 28th), because those infants were neither baptized nor catechized in the faith, yet they are accepted as martyr saints in heaven.

This is not doctrinal, however. Although there are other stories from the lives of saints that point to the possibility of those outside the faith reaching heaven.

When Anne Catherine Emmerich supposedly saw the visions of Jesus entering hell and purgatory after He was crucified to preach to the dead souls, she saw there was a hell, and then there were two other places with righteous people, one of them had pagans and the other had Jews. Jesus entered the place with the Jews and found Adam in a dark place, and he took him out of there along with others who had received God's revelation. When He entered the place with the righteous pagans and found them with demons who were forced to confess how they had deceived them with false gods, she said that it was a kind of purgatory, implying it must have only been temporary for them before they went to heaven. But this vision could possibly be wrong or invented. It was her doctor who supposedly wrote it for her.

I've wondered if maybe the way that people who die outside the church are saved could even be by missionaries being sent by the church in heaven to the souls in hell (hell in this sense being understood as like the place Abraham went to) to preach to them and baptize them there in order to bring them to heaven. The souls in mortal sin in hell hear this preaching and continue in their will to reject it, while those who died in God's grace but without the church, go to hell, hear this preaching and believe in it, so that they can leave hell and go to heaven. This is just speculation though, and obviously it might not be like this.

I've already also stated that I suspect that such people who have homosexual desires from biology really do exist, although science has failed to give conclusive proof for it. The case of Chris Birch, is a good anecdote I could point at, but it is not in itself conclusive.

The church has never stated that a single person outside of the church ever entered heaven. It has only stated that it is possible to do so, if the person was following the Truth.

If a person is born gay, I think this will be a great sign that such people saved in this way do exist, because sexuality on Earth is the reflection of the marriage in heaven.

Lord, we pray that you help all people with homosexual attractions to be reconciled with the way that you made them. Help them all to be the way that you designed them as and not the way that the world has warped them to be. We pray that all attempts to help them will be in accordance with your law and your love, and not opposed to it. We ask for these things, if it is your will, in Jesus' name, Amen

X: Same-sex parenting

This is also very controversial aspect of what is already a very controversial subject. Many same-sex couples have attempted to raise children, who they either adopted, naturally gave birth to (perhaps from a previous heterosexual relationship), or whom they used a surrogate mother or sperm donor to give birth to.

They feel, like many human beings do, a need to have a family and they do not want their sexual orientation to be a barrier to this. Against them, however, is a huge swath of society that feels like children raised in such a setting are likely to suffer psychological damage, or perhaps they are afraid the homosexual couple will abuse the children in some fashion.

Many will voice the concern that every child deserves to have both a father and mother to raise them.

There are experts doing research on the question of whether such parenting has a negative psychological effect on children or not. I am not an expert, and I can't comment too much on that issue.

The church has come out very strongly on this issue and stood in opposition to the idea of same-sex parenting. It has claimed that same-sex couples will greatly damage children by depriving them of a father or a mother figure. It is an aberration of the natural order.

Now, I feel it would be unfair if I don't mention
something here:

Consider for a moment the history of the church.

During the Middle Ages, the institution of the
monastery was at the centre of the spiritual life of
western Christendom. The Rule of St Benedict, which
itself had been re-interpreted in later ages after
Benedict died, was the most important document (after
the bible) for monastic life throughout Western Europe.
The monasteries had such a huge effect on the spiritual
life of all people in the church in the Middle Ages.

If you visit a medieval monastery still standing in
Western Europe, you sometimes may find the church is
divided into two portions. One portion was meant for
the 'choir monks' and the other portion was meant
for the 'lay monks' or 'lay brothers'. Unlike the
church today, wherein girls or boys who become nuns or
monks only do so after a discernment process to
discover their vocation, it was in fact common in the
Middle Ages for families to send their children into
monasteries while they were still children, with or
without the child's consent, and thus bind them to the
monastic vocation for the rest of their lives.

When families behaved like this, it was usually the
younger sons who were given to the church and the
older sons who inherited the property.

And throughout Europe, monasteries had no qualms about this, but they readily accepted the recruits given to them. They put them in child versions of the monastic robes, enforced corporal punishment on them to make sure they behaved well, and schooled them to be monks.

A huge number of monks of the Middle Ages were in this condition, and because they entered the monastery when they were young, therefore they received schooling in the monastery and were taught how to read and write. Most people of the society at the time were illiterate, and hence this meant that if an adult joined the monastery by his own free choice, you then often had the circumstance whereby those who had joined the monastery as children were all literate and could read the sacred scriptures, hymnals, theology books, etc. and those who joined the monastery as adults could not read any of these things, and since literacy is a harder skill to pick up for an adult than for a child, so often they were just left illiterate.

Therefore, monasteries then often had two categories of monks, who were sometimes placed into different parts of the church attached to the monastery. The 'choir monks' were those who joined as children, or who were adults of an educated background, and as their name suggests, they were the ones who formed the monastery's choir (the daily liturgy of many medieval monasteries could take many hours), whereas the 'lay brothers' were not part of the choir and

were entrusted with menial tasks and physical labour.
Often the choir monks were also ordained as priests and
the lay brothers were not.

This was a really widespread practice, all across western
Christendom. It was done with the knowledge and
approval of bishops and popes. Many saints who were
abbots engaged in this practice, and there are saints
who themselves were raised in such a way.

In the bible, Hannah gave her son Samuel to the temple
to be raised in the temple. It is possible that it was a
same-sex environment, in that only males served in the
priesthood of the temple. The Virgin Mary, according to
a tradition, was also raised for some period of her
childhood within the temple.

Thomas Aquinas, was given at the age of five by his
parents to be raised by the brothers at Monte Cassino,
and they hoped he would one day become abbot there.
Eadburh of Winchester, the daughter of Edward the Elder
of England, and who is honoured by the church as a saint,
was given by her family at a young age to monastery to
become a nun.

It is also same-sex parenting, is it not?

These boys given to the monasteries, would have
theoretically been raised in an entirely male
environment, cut off from seeing female role models,
and deprived of any mother other than the church and

the Virgin Mary. At this time, however, which pope or which bishop ever said that a great evil was being done by depriving a child of a mother or father? Who raised their voice and spoke about the abuse to the child's character that would be created by this institution? It was not just a short experiment either, but it literally lasted for centuries and encompassed the lives of thousands of people.

Catholics today speak against the horrors of same-sex parenting on the grounds that a child needs both a father and a mother, and they speak as though this was an eternal truth that the church has always held firm on, when in fact the church openly endorsed same-sex parenting for many thousands of persons in a period that lasted for centuries.

It is an eternal truth for certain, but the church has guilt in its history of failing to uphold it as well.

It is not the first time things like this have happened either, when the church militant viciously battles against something and only contradicts itself in some other time of history.

Thomas Aquinas (raised in a same-sex environment) wrote about usury and said that usury was sinful because it was the acquisition of profit without work. And people took what Aquinas said and they used this as grounds to condemn people who borrowed money on interest, who often were Jews because Jews were barred from many other kinds of work. For a long time, pious Catholics stood against this evil of usury in society and as a justification they pointed to Aquinas' words that it was immoral to earn profit without work.

In later times, when communists would attack private property and insist that the means of production belonged to the people who did work, and that the capitalists who owned the factories should not receive the fruits of the workers' labour, since they themselves did not work- to this the church stood against it and declared that labour was not the only legitimate means of attaining an income.

The irony in this was that many of the communist leaders themselves were Jews, and they were being told that this ideology was wrong because it erroneously claimed that one needed to do work in order to receive an income, when it was exactly the same argument used by Aquinas that was put down as a basis to attack those who performed usury in the Middle Ages, who were often also Jews and perhaps could have been their ancestors.

Aquinas was wrong. Acquiring a profit without work is not really what made usury sinful. What made it sinful was the fact that people would take advantage of others to essentially become debt-slaves to them for the rest of their lives through the paying of interest. If one charged interest to a person just as a means of making an income, but with the intention of trying to help the person with the loan as opposed to using the loan to make the person your debt-slave for years to come, then there is nothing wrong with this.

There's so many things like this in the church's history.

Christians refused to serve in the army of the Roman Empire on grounds that it was immoral to kill people in war and it went against the teaching of Jesus, and against this you had Pope Urban II in the 11th century calling on Christians to head to the holy land and fight the Muslims. Christians who made a vow to be crusaders and who failed to fulfill the vows could be excommunicated.

In prior ages, many Catholic bishops openly encouraged monarchs to use force to suppress the existence of other religions within their domains. Today Catholics are insisting that religious freedom is a right that must be protected.

In the 8th century, Pepin the Short wrote to Pope Zachary asking him whether it was right that the one who had the power should not also wear the crown.

Pepin the Short was the 'mayor of the palace' under the Merovingian King of the Franks. The mayor of the palace was like a military leader who had much power under the king, and Pepin essentially controlled the country, although officially he was not the king. He asked this question of Pope Zachary, almost like it was an inquiry into doctrine rather than a question of revolution.

Pope Zachary responded to him by telling him that it was right that the one who had the power should also be the one who held the crown. The Pope was not stupid, and he probably understood the reason behind the question. Pepin thus put an end to the Merovingian dynasty, forced the king to become a monk and he made himself King, creating the Carolinginan dynasty. The Pope made an alliance with this new dynasty, which he had helped create and Pepin's son, Charles the Great (Charlemagne), was crowned by the Pope as the first Holy Roman Emperor.

One thousand years later, the French revolution took place in the same country, and the Pope would be telling the people of France that they must obey their monarch and not revolt against him, because his authority was from God. And the revolutionaries would even come to Rome and kidnap the Pope, making him live a life of prayer until he died··· almost like they forced him to become a monk.

The Pope was right, the one who held the power should

be the one who held the crown; the Lord speaks through bishops, but what He means could be different from what they intended to say; if we follow the bishop, then we are led astray, but if we follow the Person who speaks through him and put the law of God and the gospel first, then we will not be led astray. The correct application of this teaching would be for Pepin to surrender his power to the king, rather than the king surrendering his throne to Pepin. And so, the one who held the power then would be the one who had the crown.

In the 19th century, there was a Catholic maidservant to a Jewish family in the Papal states, and she saw their young son was sick and might die. She was afraid he would die and go to hell, so she baptized him without the parents' knowledge. The child recovered and did not die. And the maidservant told others about what she had done.

In the laws of the Papal States, non-Christian parents were not permitted to raise a Christian child. So, the child was taken away from the family. Pius IX, the pope at the time, fully supported this and in fact arranged for the child to be raised within the papal household; which perhaps was also a same-sex environment. The parents came to plead to have their boy back, but the Pope refused and stood by his decision. Even prominent catholic leaders like Emperor Napoleon III of France would call on the Pope to change his mind. But the Pope believed he did nothing wrong.

In the 21st century, Catholic voices complain about governments interfering with the raising of their children and teach that the rights of the family precede the rights of the state.

When faced with this situation, the church's teaching comes first and the bishop comes second. The church teaching is that the rights of the family precede the rights of the state, meaning the Pope had no right to remove the child from his parents against their consent on these grounds. The Pope had a good intention, which was to give the Christian faith to the child, but this method was not licit in the church's teaching. If he really required the child to receive the Christian faith, then he could have simply mandated that the parents would allow the child to receive religious instruction, while they retained possession of the child.

I wonder if perhaps the loss of the territory of the Papal States within the reign of the same Pope was not in fact a punishment from God for this kind of abuse of temporal power.

Catholics may not think like this, but God remains the same even when the church is inconsistent. Popes, bishops, priests and the laity can all be misled, and the church militant can in fact stand and fight something in one age, and support it in another age, but God is always the same God. His law and His gospel are always the same. He will punish His children, because He loves them as a parent, and He will remind the church through His Spirit of what He came down to the Earth to teach.

If we follow idols, then we should believe the people; if we follow God, then we know the people are guides that point us to Him, and not the end in themselves, which means everything they teach can only be understood correctly in reference to His teaching.

There is in fact so much material and information within the church which is assumed to be from God, but actually is just from human beings, albeit human beings who are filled with God's Spirit.

The Church is always right because the Church is from God. It was not wrong to live on income that didn't come from work in the industrial revolution, nor was it wrong to do so in the Middle Ages – it was human thinking that made people think that this was the reason for the Church's teachings against usury.

Fighting in self-defence against an enemy who is invading was morally acceptable. It was morally acceptable to fight in a necessary self-defence against Muslims just as it was morally acceptable to fight to defend the Roman state from invaders. It was human thinking that made people think that fighting in war was necessarily evil; fighting in a war was not morally impossible for that reason, but it was morally impossible for other reasons. It was morally impossible because the soldiers would be required to do evil things by their commanders in the course of the war and not all wars were fought for just reasons - but that truth applied to Christian armies and crusaders just as it did to the roman army.

Religious liberty is something that ought to be given to Catholics today, just as it ought to have been given to Protestants and Jews living in Catholic countries hundreds of years previously.

The church is filled with human thinking that masks itself as though it were from God. Many Catholics speak for the church without logic and in the end, they only mask the Church's true glory and wisdom.

When the Kentucky clerk Kim Davis was arrested for refusing to grant marriage licenses to gay couples in 2015, there were many Catholics who openly supported her, while at the same time criticizing the German bishops who wanted to alter the church's practices regarding communion for remarried persons or homosexuals.

Ms. Davis was divorced and remarried three times, and

if she was living in a state of grace, then Cardinal Kasper and the German bishops must therefore have been correct when they said that such people were not necessarily living in mortal sin. If the German bishops were apostates to the faith for saying that such people could be in a state of grace, then all these Catholics defending Ms. Davis must have been apostates too for claiming she was living her life for God if they also knew that she had been divorced and remarried.

If the church can be divided in two by a schism for the past thousand years and the whole church fails to solve the problem, when you in fact know for certain that the Holy Spirit's will is for unity, you don't need more evidence than this in order to know that a huge amount of what happens in the church is not actually done according to the Holy Spirit's suggestion.

The Holy Spirit rules the church through suggestions and as a friend, not as master to a slave. He does not control the bishops and laity as though they were His robots to order about as He willed. He gives them suggestions and they can say yes or no, and He does not force Himself upon people who are not willing to accept what He asks for.

So, when confronted with this issue of children being raised by gay couples, if we were to attack the idea of it

on the principle that a child should have both a father
and a mother, then logically we must also condemn the
history of the church along with it as well. So, what do
we do? Do we say that the church was right in all of
those centuries and that we will let go of this principle
we argue upon to attack gay parenting, or do we
condemn the church of that period and the same-sex
parenting together?

It goes back to the question again, of whether we follow
the people or we follow God, the idol or the Creator.

It is not the example of the saints that creates church
doctrine. The clergy, even the Pope, only have the
power to interpret doctrine and not create or change it.
Christ Himself did not have the authority to change
what He was commanded to say or do by the Father.
God's law remains true in every age regardless of what
the clergy or the saints do or say. Hence, if natural laws
tells us that a child needs both a father and a mother,
then same-sex parenting is wrong and so was the
practice of the church of the Middle Ages also wrong.

Today, you may still find catholic orphanages perhaps
run entirely by nuns, and this must also be condemned
for the same reason. The orphanage is a good thing, and
they are doing a good work, but they ought to be
obliged to find males who will be parents to the orphans
with the nuns.

What damage does this practice do to children, however? I am not a psychologist, nor have I studied this topic, but it would be interesting to know how an orphan raised exclusively by catholic nuns or how a boy given to a monastery is mentally affected by same-sex parenting.

I don’t know if this anecdote is worth anything or not, but I will repeat it here:

A famous story about Thomas Aquinas holds that when he was a young person he made a decision to join the Dominicans (as opposed to becoming abbot of Monte Cassino or some other monastery, as his parents originally planned). His parents were so upset by this, because of the scandal involved in the idea that their boy would become a mendicant friar (which was not held in respect as an Abbot of an established monastery was). So, they imprisoned him in the family castle for almost a year. During this time, one of Thomas’ family members decided to try to bring a prostitute into his room to seduce him, but Thomas used tongs to take a hot iron from the fire and threatened he would burn her with it if she didn’t leave, in order to keep his purity intact. She left and he kept his purity intact.

If we contrast this story for a moment with a different saint: John of the Cross, unlike Thomas Aquinas who was from nobility, came from a poor family of weavers, who descended from converted Spanish Jews. He was raised as a normal child in a family, and not in the same-sex environment of a monastery. He became a Carmelite in his 20s and joined Teresa's reform movement, which he remained part of for the rest of his life. There is a story about him very similar to the story about Aquinas, wherein a woman came to him when he was a friar and announced her love for him. He did not take a weapon in his hand to scare her away, but told her in a kind and sensitive manner that he couldn't have that love with her and she left.

This anecdote proves nothing, I think. It may easily be the case the prostitute would keep trying to seduce Aquinas unless she was threatened like that, and John of the Cross would have treated her the same way if he had run across someone like her, and the woman he met was not like her at all.

But I just imagine that Aquinas' and others like him probably did not have the same view on males and females as normal people did, because of the upbringing they went through. If children raised in same-sex households today suffer damage to their characters or worldviews from the lack of a mother or father figure, then surely many of the monks of the Middle Ages must have had something similar.

Many of the saints of the Middle Ages were either people like Aquinas who were raised in this abnormal setting, or who joined monasteries as adults and were taught or influenced by people who themselves were raised in this setting. Hence this abnormal setting actually had a rather significant influence on the development of the church.

It is worth wondering how the church would have developed differently if this hadn't all happened.

Universally enforced priestly celibacy was greatly linked with the reform movements that stemmed from monasteries in the Middle Ages, the thinking of the church towards who God is, what sin is, heaven and hell, the relation of the church to heretics, the relation of the church to other religions, the mercy and justice of God⋯ for all of these things the church for the rest of its history would receive very heavy influence from the writings and minds of men whose faith was heavily influenced by an institution (the monastery) that formed a great deal of its membership through same-sex parenting.

If the church is right and same-sex parenting has the potential to damage the psychology, character or worldview of a person, then surely the church itself must ask the question as to how much of the church's own collective psychology, character or worldview was malformed as a result of institutionalized same-sex parenting within the monasteries that formed the heart of Medieval Christendom.

However, we cannot condemn the church too harshly

when it did this in the Middle Ages. They had their own reasons for why they carried out this practice.

Odo of Cluny, when he was a monk and still not an abbot, once visited a noble family who had a daughter that was engaged to be married. The daughter privately begged Odo to save her from the marriage and let her join a monastery. He then took her from her home, without her parent's knowledge or consent, and brought her back to his monastery. The abbot (Berno of Cluny) was going to punish him, and Odo repented of his sins, but said he had done so because he needed to save the girl's soul. Perhaps in his thinking, and the thinking of many of the reformed monks of the Middle Ages, there was essentially no salvation outside of the monastery, except for very few.

Today, many people in the church think that those in other religions are saved just like Catholics, but the church does not teach this. If anyone is saved in other religions it can only be through the church, as a catechumen who has not yet been baptized. Similarly, if people are saved outside the monasteries, it is only because they are also living a life with a close relationship to God, just as those in the monasteries do.

In our times people think that all are saved, including those outside the church, and at that time people thought that outside the monasteries, few were saved.

At that time, the pendulum was in the opposite direction, and the monks who influenced the rest of the church thought that almost no one in the church was saved except for the monks, even though the church never taught that it was almost impossible to be saved outside of a monastic life. Hence, the tendency they had to try to reform the church as a monastery, according to their own upbringing and experience, then comes from this form of thinking.

The child who is given to the monastery was deprived of a normal family, however, the child was assured of salvation in the monastery, or at least they thought he was, whereas in the world there were too many temptations and things that could draw the soul down to hell. Of course, being raised in a monastery would be a better choice over a family that would allow the child to be corrupted and go down to hell, because no matter what psychological harm was done by the family when it deprived them of a normal parentage it is still not as great a harm as is done by corrupting a child's morals and leading them to hell.

They assumed that outside the monastery was a place without safety for a soul, and therefore any child given to them they assumed to be in better hands than if they left them within the world.

Whether right or wrong, this was the thinking they probably possessed.

Under this lens, we can then discuss the morality of

whether same-sex parents can raise children. A homosexual couple, because the nature of their relationship is gravely sinful, could not possibly be said to be a good moral example for children. Hence, the logic that was used by medieval monks to deprive children of normal families with a father and mother could not be used here.

If the homosexual couple abstained from all sexual activity and they lived together as two brothers or two sisters, and provided a very good moral example to the children in question, like monks or nuns, then this would not be such a great evil, and it would be better than many families in existence that allow or cause the morals of their children to be corrupted. If you had a same-sex couple who abstained from all sexual activity and gave the children a good moral example, taught them to pray and helped them to get to heaven, this would still be a better place for a child than many heterosexual couples who engage in sins and teach their children to sin, and bring them to hell. Damage is being done by depriving them of a father or a mother, but it is still not as bad as the damage of sending the child to hell.

So, should same-sex parenting exist or not then?

There still shouldn’t be any at all. Because even if you had a same-sex couple who really did abstain from all sex and live together as Mary and Joseph, or more rather like Berno or Odo and their monks, and gave a good moral example to the children they were raising... such a couple still ought to find a member of the opposite sex to raise the child with them. The monasteries of the Middle Ages should have done so as well.

The same is also true of single parents; if a single mom is able to get a father figure for her child or children to help raise them, even if this person is not her husband, this is preferable than just her raising the child on her own. And for single fathers, vice-versa.

For that matter, one could also include in this list the many heterosexual parents who are simply not present in the lives of their children and leave the other parent to do most of the work of raising the children.

Even if what I suggest as possible is actually the truth, and people born homosexual are heterosexual in disguise, and even if a sexual complementarity could exist in a same-sex couple (which is not actually same-sex, because one of them is the opposite sex in disguise), I am not sure that this kind of parenting would be acceptable.

This is because, at least as I understand it, the child is learning gender roles from their parents, and a person who is a man or woman in many ways except their sexuality, is not really going to teach their sons or daughters about the opposite sex by their behaviour, even should they themselves be the opposite sex in disguise.

If the person has the soul of the opposite sex, and most of their body (excepting part of the brain) appears like it is of their own seeming sex, even if you gave the person hormones and 'transitioned' them, I think they still will not fully master the traditional gender roles of a man or a woman, hence, for that reason they perhaps would not be the right people for the children to learn these gender roles from.

Lord, we pray that all children will receive a good upbringing and have all their needs fulfilled. We pray that all parents everywhere will provide a good moral example to their children, and that children will be protected from all kinds of deception from adults that would corrupt their morals concerning human sexuality. We ask for these things, if it is your will, in Jesus' name, Amen

XI: Transgender

In the teaching tradition of the church, I could be wrong, but I think there has never been a magisterial document that ever addressed this issue directly.

There are magisterial statements that condemn the viewpoint that gender is decided by human beings and there are statements that say we must accept the gender God gave to us, but in itself that does not negate transgenderism, it would simply mean that gender is decided by God and not by human beings- a transgendered person who believed that God decided for them to be a member of the opposite sex and that by believing they were a member of the opposite sex, they were accepting the gender God gave to them, would not be in contradiction with this doctrine in theory.

There are some in the clergy who have preached or written about this topic, and the Lord will help guide their teaching because of the office they hold, but their words do not make something into doctrine.

As Catholics, we believe that it is the magisterium and not the priest at the pulpit that has the authority to define what is and what is not correct doctrine. And that is only to define it; it has no power at all to change or create it. The priest at the pulpit has the authority to teach this doctrine, but not to define it for the larger church. It is rather the role of the Popes and church councils to do that.

And such doctrine cannot be understood correctly without the Person who stands behind it and the light of His gospel.

When Galileo was tried, the clergy who were against him were simply assuming that the church taught that the Earth was the centre of the universe. They assumed this, but they were wrong. If Galileo had asked them to reference some document from a council or pope to back up their charges against him that this was a heresy, they would have been left without a case, because such documents never existed. Perhaps people assumed that they did, but that assumption was wrong.

The people who tried Galileo referenced the bible and some church fathers in order to back up their claims about this being correct doctrine. However, not everything that the church fathers wrote is accepted by the church to be true, and their own interpretations of the bible were also fallible, and hence they didn't really have a magisterial backing to their claim that a geocentric universe was correct doctrine.

Many times in the history of the church, people assume that the church teaches something that it doesn't. Sometimes even the church struggles very hard and many people stand militantly in defence of church teaching against the society, because they have been led to believe that the church teaches something that it in fact doesn't.

The case of church teaching on other religions is such a strong example on that matter.

At the time of the French revolution, many faithful Catholics in France believed that the church taught that Protestants should not have equal civil rights with Catholics. They thought this way because many in the clergy themselves promoted this kind of thinking.

Since the start of the Reformation, Protestants in France were treated with violence (particularly in the wars of religion) and by discrimination in society in many forms including within the law itself. And this discrimination was openly supported by many priests and bishops in France from whom the faithful learned the gospel.

Jacques-Bénigne Bossuet (1627-1704), bishop of Meaux wrote "Those who maintain that the prince should not use force in matters of religion, for the reason that religion should be free, are in an impious error" [2]

Étienne Charles de Loménie de Brienne (1727-1794), archbishop of Toulouse told King Louis XVI on his coming to the throne in 1775, "We conjure you, Sire, do not take delay to take from error the hope of having among us temples and altars. It is reserved for you to strike the last blow to Calvinism in your dominions. Order the dispersion of the schismatic meetings of the Protestants; exclude

---

[2] John P. Lacroix, Religion and the Reign of Terror. 1869, New York. Carlton and Lanahan. P30

them, without distinction, from all public functions, and you will assure to your subjects the unity of Christian worship." [3]

When new laws allowing greater 'toleration' (not complete legal equality) were being discussed shortly prior to the revolution, Jean-Jacques Duval d'Eprémesnil (1745-1794) in the Parliament of Paris held up a picture of Christ's face and shouted out, "Would you crucify Him again?" [4]

The Assembly of the Clergy in 1788 called on the King to revoke the Edict of Toleration. This was the last thing this assembly did before the revolution started.

The clergy who were gathered made this statement: "This sect, which in the midst of its ruins preserves the spirit of audacity and independence with which it has shown from the beginning, wishes to arrogate for falsehood the rights which only belong to the truth···This sect presumes to demand a civil and religious existence; hence the necessity of vigorously resisting all of its efforts" [5]

---

[3] John P. Lacroix, Religion and the Reign of Terror. 1869, New York. Carlton and Lanahan. P43

[4] John P. Lacroix, Religion and the Reign of Terror. 1869, New York. Carlton and Lanahan. P43

[5] John P. Lacroix, Religion and the Reign of Terror. 1869, New York. Carlton and Lanahan. P43

In the end it was they, the catholic clergy, who would be subject to persecution they were calling for, rather than the Protestants.

When the Catholics in France at that time came to think that the church was fundamentally against equal rights to Protestants, whose fault was this really? They were disobeying the law written on the human heart in order to follow the words of those who held Christ's authority. They were following the creature in place of the Creator who spoke through the creature.

If someone from our times went back in time and showed the people living then the ecumenism that began after the Second Vatican Council, the various magisterial documents being made about rights to religious freedom and respect for not only protestants, but other religions that honoured God… the people living then perhaps could not believe that this was the same church.

At this time period, there were people in the United States (including freemasons among them) who created a new form of government that embraced all these ideas that the bishops in France were decrying. Freedom of religion, freedom of speech, freedom to publish, etc. At the time, it was the protestant and masonic 'enemies' of the church, those whom were condemned by the Pope, that were teaching these things, while there were bishops telling people that God rejected such ideas and it was a sin to believe in them. As the bishop of Meaux said: 'an impious error'.

Devout Catholics in France living then could have understood these principles in the United States as though they were errors that came from the devil, because they thought that the Catholic Church taught that these things were errors.

When d'Eprémesnil held up the picture of Christ's face to those calling for equal rights for Protestants and called out 'Would you crucify him again?' could he be blamed for thinking like this? Was he not just following what the clergy were saying to the sheep they were entrusted with?

If at that time period you claimed that the enemies of the church were right and that the state couldn＇t use force against people to eliminate religious minorities outside of the church, you would perhaps be branded as uncatholic. Do you follow what the protestants and free masons are saying in America, do you follow what these anti-church radicals are saying in France, or do you follow the teachings of the bishops?

And yet the church two centuries later would claim that freedom of religion was a natural right of human beings given from God and complain about governments that infringed this right.

Not long ago, there was an infamous case of blasphemy in Paris when a play performed had the actors throwing feces at an image of Christ's face. It is just my imagination, but I couldn't help but feel reminded of the church's actions in that place centuries past. Who was really the one who blasphemed Christ's face more, was it these actors or was it d'Eprémesnil? And was it really d'Eprémesnil or was it the clergy who taught him?

The patron saint of France, Joan of Arc in her death had something worth contemplating on this point. She was tried by the inquisition and sentenced to death. The bishop told her that she could not believe that her visions were from a holy origin. What should she do, follow the authority of the bishop, on whom Christ's authority rested or follow her visions and die excommunicated?

When Christ was being tried before Caiaphas and Annas, and both condemned him, who were the Jews supposed to listen to? Didn't God give his authority over questions of religion to the High Priest? Didn't they have the authority to tell people whether or not the faithful were permitted to follow this man?

But really, what is the correct answer to this question? Does it mean that it is in fact possible for the faithful to know better than the church about what is right and what is wrong? Does it mean that the voice of the bishops can be ignored and rejected?

I would argue that the answer is still no.

The people who wrote those things above were bishops, and people had an obligation to listen to their teaching because they were bishops. Part of the mystery of the sacrament of Holy Orders is that the Holy Spirit guides the bishop in his teaching to protect it from leading the faithful astray.

Were people led astray by this, however?

The truth is that there is a certain moral danger in treating other religions, even those that worship Christ, as though they were equal to the true church founded by Jesus Christ. Hence, it cannot be said that the Holy Spirit was not present and using the bishops to keep people away from making errors, for it is indeed an error to think that Protestantism and Catholicism are equivalent and should be treated the same.

Furthermore, it is also an error to suggest that the state has no role in helping to differentiate between what is true and what is false, and to keep people away from ideas which would hurt them. This means that it is not a mistake to teach that the state has a duty to try to use its resources to protect people from following false doctrines in other religions.

The Holy Spirit is still present and still teaching through these bishops. But the way that the faithful came to understand this, in thinking that Protestants must be treated badly and not allowed to worship under the law is an idea that is ultimately a mistake. And they thought this way because they were following the bishops and not thinking of the gospel of the One who spoke through them.

They were many ideas within the French revolution that were very dangerous to society and which have filled the world today, and have been the source of much moral relativism. Not all religions are equal, not all opinions are equally valid, not everyone should have a right to publish or preach any idea at all, and it is not the case that the state has no right to make rules over such things.

But what you saw at this time in the 18th century in France was that the Catholic Church, speaking of its membership rather than its magisterial authority, mostly understood that the Catholic Church taught that Protestants could not be given equal rights under the law.

The magisterium had never explicitly stated as a moral teaching that Protestants or people of other religions should not be allowed to worship legally or that they were supposed to be treated badly or with unfair discrimination by the state. People perhaps just assumed that it had, but they were wrong. Even though people throughout the church, including saints, priests, bishops and Popes may have thought like this, without the church ever defining such a doctrine, it is ultimately just an assumption and not a doctrine.

The assumption was based on a true principle, and one which the Holy Spirit used the bishops to teach, which was that Protestantism and Catholicism could not be treated as though they were the same, and the state had a responsibility to try to help people to differentiate correctly so that they didn't fall into error and to help those who had fallen into error to come to the Truth.

In cases where public morals or safety is threatened by some religious body, the state can even use force if necessary; the teaching of those bishops is not false on this point- it is indeed an impious error to assert that force cannot be used in matters of religion if a religious body is threatening the moral or physical safety of the public. This doesn't, however, mean that every religious body that thinks differently from the Church is thereby a threat to public morals and safety that requires force. This applies to the Catholic Church, however, just as much as it does to Protestants. If Catholics were threatening the moral or physical safety of people in society, the state would also have a right to use force against the Church.

The Spirit, while using the bishops to teach these things, did not tell them that this meant that they had to violate the teaching example of Christ who rebuked His disciples when they asked if fire should come down on the Samaritans who didn't accept Him. They did not know which spirit they were following. He came into the world to save the world, not to condemn it. Similarly, people in the church also did not realize which spirit they were following when they made this error, even though the error was based in something true, when they concluded that those who did not accept the church teachings were supposed to be destroyed or suppressed.

The voice of the Church must always be trusted. However, that doesn't mean that those outside the church are always wrong. It does occur that people outside sometimes understand aspects of the gospel better than many members of the church do.

You must always trust the voice of the church, but everything that the church says can only be correctly understood under the light of the Sacred Heart of Jesus. People in the past church were led astray, not because they were following the voice of the bishops, to whom they must always listen to, but because they were not listening to the Person speaking through the voice of the bishops, and interpreting their teachings with reference to His gospel.

The French revolutionaries were violent atheists who attacked the church and persecuted it. They had ideas which were rejected by Catholics at the time, and yet some of which were later embraced by the church of the 20th and 21st centuries, because the church never truly taught the things that people had assumed it did.

In our time, we see a very sinful homosexual subculture that parades and promotes all sorts of perversions, and it attacks the church, perhaps not violently, but still wishing to attack its status and influence in society. However, it may be the case that there are ideas they have, which are rejected by most Catholics now but which are not actually incorrect, and do not contradict church teaching, because the church doesn't actually teach as people think it does.

In the question of whether a man can be born in a woman's body or a woman in a man's, are we facing something similar to this or not?

The church magisterial teaching has never told people that transgenderism is sinful. The catechism itself doesn't even mention it, oddly enough, despite the fact that this is a clearly a moral issue that confronts people in the modern world.

However, if one were to ask Catholics what they thought, I think that a large body of them, including priests and bishops, would all say that it was sinful and cannot be accepted. However, their opinions do not have the authority to define doctrines.

No matter who says it, how many people say it, etc. it ultimately doesn't stand as an authority that must be fully trusted until the Holy Spirit says it through the Magisterium.

The church has never defined what it is in the human being that makes a person a male or a female. I already wrote about this above in the chapter about being born gay.

If it were the DNA or the sex organs that define gender, then we can find women with male DNA and born with internal testes with no ovaries.

If you were to take the personality of the person as the definition, you would run into problems with this as well. There are men who possess traditionally feminine attributes in their personality, but who are still essentially men. There are women who possess traditionally masculine attributes in their personality, but who are still essentially women.

There are men who are good with children and women who are not. There are women who have interests in engines and machines, and there are men who have interests in interior decorating or fashion; these interests do not define their sex.

There are men who giggle. There are women who grunt. There are women who think very rationally, and men who think very emotionally. But, these things do not define their sex.

There are men who are very good at making relationships with people, there are women who are autistic and can't make relationships with people. These things do not define their sex.

There are women who are emotionally strong, and there are men who easily cry. These things do not define their sex.

Name any traditionally feminine or masculine attribute that you like, and you will find that there are exceptions to it somewhere with someone. Any traditional feminine attribute, you can find a man somewhere who has it, even if most men do not. Any traditional masculine attribute, you can find a woman somewhere who has it, even if most women do not.

Hence, anyone who tries to define gender on the basis of these things, and insist that a person is a man or a woman because of these things in their personality, is ultimately making a mistake.

I think that God perhaps intended it to be like this and to create such exceptions in order to prevent people from defining gender on these bases.

The church has never defined what part of the person makes a man a man or a woman a woman.

However, the church doesn’t ‘create’ doctrines when it defines doctrines. When the magisterium defines doctrines, it is only just providing explanation and clarification to what has already been revealed in Christ. It doesn’t change teaching or create new teachings, but it does change how people understand teaching and tells them things about the teaching that they didn’t understand before.

I believe that the deposit of faith has everything inside of it needed in order to understand what the correct teaching of this must be.

This is because while the church has not spoken about what makes a man a man or a woman a woman, it has explicitly stated that homosexuality is a disordered condition and not the way that God made people.

If this is true, then it must logically follow that if anyone was created by God with a natural sexual orientation towards males then this person must be a female, and if towards females, then this person must be a male. It must be like this, otherwise the church is wrong and God does in fact make people this way.

All of those other attributes, including the DNA, the sex organs, the outward body, even all those personality traits... none of these things define gender. It is the sexual preference assigned by the person＇s biology which must be the thing that defines gender.

The church does not say that a man who likes watching teary soap operas is disordered. The church does not say that a woman who loves weapons and military things is disordered. The church does not say that men who cry when their wives bully them are disordered. The church does not say that women who have no desires for giving birth to children are disordered.

The church, however, does say that a person who has a sexual attraction to the same sex is disordered.

Take any feminine attribute you like, and if a woman doesn＇t have it, she is still a woman and the church teaching is not broken. Take any masculine attribute you like, and if a man doesn＇t have it, he is still a man and the church teaching is not broken. But you can＇t say that a man is designed for a man or a woman is designed for a woman; for if you do so, then the church＇s teaching is broken. This is the part of the person that must define the gender of their soul.

All the answers to the questions of doctrine are already revealed, we just need to look more studiously at the deposit of faith under the light of the One it came from in order to find them. The church does not create new doctrines, it merely explains things that were not understood before.

However, as I mentioned earlier, the first explanation remains possible and it still may be the case that all homosexuality is psychological only, in which case there is no hidden gender.

On that note, however, the church has never stated that there was ever a person outside the church who got to heaven. The catechism merely says that if someone outside the church is seeking the Truth and living by it, he can be counted as baptized… it doesn't say whether or not such a person has ever or ever will exist, however – the catechism's statement could be referring to something entirely hypothetical. I and many others have assumed that such people do exist, but the church has never once said that they do, it has only defined what the conditions are for them to find salvation.

If a person is born homosexual, then I think this will be a great sign that such people do in fact exist outside the church, because human sexuality is the mirror of the marriage in heaven.

Lord, we pray that you help us and help the church to understand your plans for the world better as it

concerns these issues. We pray for clarity regarding
these issues and that we will not be led into deception
concerning them. We pray that all people will accept
and acknowledge the gender that you gave to them at
their creation and be comfortable with it. We pray that
you help especially all those who struggle with
accepting their gender to find peace in accepting how
you made them to be. We pray that you help them to
avoid any behaviour which is harmful to themselves. We
ask for these things, if it is your will, in Jesus' name,
Amen

XII: Transgender Transitioning:

When speaking of transgendered people, however,
there a large number of people who identify themselves
as transgendered but who are sexually attracted to the
opposite-sex (opposite to their biological sex). If we take
what I wrote above as true, then it must be the case
that these people are not born in the wrong body,
because God does not make anyone gay.

They may feel extremely uncomfortable about their
gender, and they feel so much happier trying to live as
the opposite sex, but they still are not the opposite sex,
because God does not make anyone gay.

Something needs to be said here, which is really important that I write, to make sure that no one is harmed by this book.

<u>The question of whether or not a person can actually be transgendered, and the question of whether or not they should try to 'transition' into the opposite sex are two completely different questions.</u>

I think that it makes perfect sense to determine gender on the basis of the sexual orientation assigned by the person's neural biology, because the church's own teaching would deny the possibility that God created a person with a homosexual orientation. Hence, if the way that God created a person is in fact with feelings towards the same sex, then it must be that the true gender is not what it looks like. Rejection of the body is rejection of the Creator, and the brain is part of the body.

If the personality of the person in life is a mistake, because the brain is not the way it was supposed to be, then where exactly is the person anymore?

Allow me to illustrate what I mean.

For example, since I was a child I had a very strong interest in history, politics, geography and all sorts of things relating to the way that societies worked. This interest led me to pursue it in so many ways, whether in my schooling, my hobbies, my conversations with people, my writings, my prayers, my meditations, and my relationship with God. I have a profound feeling that the mystery of my life surrounds the question of whether all the things that happen in this world really have a Person behind them or not.

I don' t think I would be the same person without these interests. But let us suppose I die and meet God in heaven, and He tells me that this was just a big mistake, because my neural biology was supposed to be this way and not that way, and so I had this lifelong interest was just because of an error in neural biology and all this stuff that this interest created in my life and personality was just a giant error. Then the Lord tells me, I was actually supposed to be an ice cream salesman and to have Interests in hockey and sporting events, but because of this error in my neural biology that led me to develop different interests, none of that happened.

Does this seem conceivable?

But if we are really going to believe like the neural biology of the person is a mistake, and that the personality created by this biology is a mistake and that all the thoughts and feelings of the person were all distorted because of it... then that must be a possibility.

If it is possible that the person who is essentially born with this orientation, the personality he develops and all the thoughts and feelings he develops in his life, was just a big mistake... then equally we should just as easily be able to say that the woman who went through life absorbed in her children's lives might also be a giant mistake because perhaps God planned her personality to be different and she was supposed to be a reclusive scientist... then equally we should be able to say that the man who spent much of his life with feelings of profound regret over injustices in the world was never supposed to have these feelings, because of some error in his neural biology, and in fact he was supposed to be a great lover of music and cats.

Ultimately the final question we get down to is essentially this: is God in control of this world or not?

If the answer is yes, then it is inconceivable to conclude that these things are feasible. How could it possibly be that these people die and go to heaven, and God then takes away their personality and changes them into something they never felt, never knew and never were in their lives on Earth, because what happened on Earth was operating outside of His plan?

Sexual orientation is also not an insignificant part of a person. It is not the whole person, but only part of the person, however, it is an important part.

To suggest that a person whose neural biology gives them this orientation, and their interests, personality and thoughts and feelings throughout their lives is just a giant mistake, I think is essentially to deny that God is in control of this world.

When people go to heaven, when they resurrect on the last day, they will have the same personalities as they do now. There are many things in our psychologies that were perhaps warped by being present in a sinful world filled with suffering and away from God, and in this way someone can perhaps 'change' their personality once they get to heaven, not because it really changes, but because it is being restored to what it was supposed to be in the original.

All of the desires you had for things that were bad, you will find that they were actually desires for a good, desires for God, but they only desired evil because the good was not present. However, they were the same desires, and you will not get new ones when you enter into eternal life; you will rather just see what the true object of your desires was all along.

There are perhaps things that God will give to people in their personalities in addition to what they had in life. Such that the person born with Down syndrome perhaps will possess both the personality with the

Down syndrome and what they would have been without it, or the person born in a vegetative state will possess both the vegetative state and the animated state, etc.

Although I don't know if my assumptions about the resurrection are all true, I would point out, as a supporting piece of evidence, that Isaiah said that the blind shall see and the deaf shall hear.

But even should this happen, and they are thus given something new that they didn't have before, they will still be the same people ultimately and what they had in life is still part of them forever, but in a glorified form, free from suffering, and restored to its original perfection.

I think that so many people in religious communities fight against the idea that homosexuality is created by God because they feel like it is proving their religions wrong, when in fact the exact opposite is true. If the things religion teaches is not found in the real world itself, but only in an abstract idea known because of faith, then there is nothing else that could disprove religion more than this.

The things that the church teaches are proven true because they can be found in the real world. This is because the same God who created the world is the same God who gave the church its teachings. What He tells us through the church is borne up and proven to be true by the experience of people within His creation.

If, however, we say that the whole world can really be outside of God's hands like this; that the life and personality of the individual from beginning to end can be so completely disjointed from how God planned the person to be, then what religion says essentially has no meaning over the real world as it actually exists.

But this is not the case. God does rule this world and the life of each individual is in His hands. The personality He gives to people in this world shall belong to them forever. Perhaps there are additional things that can be given to a person in heaven in addition to what they had in life, but what they had in life will still forever be part of who they are.

Now, here is an important thing that needs to be said to make sure no one takes this book and does something harmful with it.

Because of everything I just wrote above, the idea that someone needs to reject themselves and change in order to become more like members of the opposite sex is an idea which must be completely condemned.

If everything I wrote above is correct, then it is wrong for a person to reject the body they are made with or the personality they were made with, and to try to artificially get a new body or a new personality.

If it is possible for the brain to be wrong; if it is possible for the person to be born with a neural biology that makes him homosexual, and this is all a mistake and not God's handiwork, then in truth, there is no reason why we should condemn transsexualism. Because if the brain can be wrong, then the whole body can be wrong, and if the personality of the person is a mistake because the brain is a mistake, then perhaps the masculinity of femininity of a person can be a mistake as well.

But this is wrong. Rejection of the body or the personality is rejection of the Creator. Rejection of yourself is rejection of God.

The deception of the devil is so powerful, and without light it is so difficult to see in the darkness.

Even if what I write above is true and the person born with the homosexual attraction is actually the opposite sex in disguise, this person is still who he is and he should not try to change who he is to become a different person.

The key point in all of this is that he must be himself, and he must accept himself as he is.

If a boy, regardless of whether he be homosexual or heterosexual, has an interest in feminine things, likes things that girls like and he acts in ways that are often considered feminine, because that is what he wants to do, then there is nothing wrong with this in itself. And vice-versa for a girl, regardless of whether she be homosexual or heterosexual.

All that I said before about cross-dressing would apply to this, however, in that they must still be mindful of offending people, indulging in anything sexual or creating unnecessary scandal.

If the boy likes feminine things or likes to behave in a way that is considered feminine, because that is who he is, then there is nothing wrong with this. Furthermore, if that is his true interests as God gave him, then they are ultimately masculine interests, even if human beings would normally think of them as feminine interests. It is not human beings who have the right to decide what truly constitutes femininity or masculinity, and God is not bound by human definitions for when he gives the gift of gender.

This is different, however, from a boy who pursues feminine things and tries to act in a feminine way, not because that is what he wants to do or because it is the interests that he has naturally, but because he is uncomfortable with who he is and who wants to pursue these things out of this discomfort.

He pursues things he has no interest in, because those

things are feminine things and he feels that he needs to be a girl to be comfortable with himself. He does things that he doesn't really want to do, because those things are feminine things and he needs to be a girl to be comfortable with himself.

This is a disordered condition; he is rejecting his own identity in order to be something that he is not, because he feels uncomfortable with the identity that he has.

And vice-versa for girls that pursue masculine things out of discomfort over their own selves.

The key point in all of this is that he must be himself. If a boy (whether homosexual or heterosexual) acts like a girl and pursues interests in things that girls have interests in, because that is what feels right to him, that is how his personality actually is, then there is nothing wrong with this, so long he does so in a way that is mindful to try to avoid offending people and the other commandments are also kept. This is OK, because he is being himself by doing these things and is doing what the catechism demands, which is that each person must accept their own sexual identity.

If God designed a boy to have an interest in ballet, and he rejects this interest to suit what other people define masculinity ought to be, he is ultimately rejecting God's design in favour of human thinking. To be interested in ballet, for him, is a masculine interest, even if the world would think otherwise and it is part of a masculine vocation in this life

Louis XIV was a ballet dancer and loved ballet. There is a famous image of him as a young man dressed as the Greek god Apollo in a ballet he danced in. He wasn't homosexual or transgender – he slept around with many women in his life, beyond his wife and had illegitimate children. This interest was a part of his masculinity.

If God designed a girl to have an interest in military fighting, and she rejects this interest to suit what other people define femininity ought to be, she is ultimately rejecting God's design in favour of human thinking. To be interested in military fighting, for her, is a feminine interest, even if the world would think otherwise and it is part of a feminine vocation in this life.

Joan of Arc served as a soldier in war at God's calling. She referred to herself as a daughter of God and obediently listened to His voice as the woman she was when He instructed her to go to war. This was part of her feminine vocation.

People have to accept the natures that God gave them; they cannot redefine their genders according to human thinking about what gender ought to be.

But the same logic also applies to people who reject their own genders out of discomfort. If a boy can't stand being a boy, so he stops doing the things that he is interested in and he starts pursuing things that girls are interested in, but which he actually is not interested in, he is ultimately rejecting the nature that God gave him in order to suit his own discomfort. It is also a rejection of nature and a rejection of the One who gifted that nature.

If he feels uncomfortable with himself, even profoundly uncomfortable with himself, unless he does things he doesn't really want to do and pursues things that he doesn't actually have an interest in, the problem that needs to be corrected is not his gender but rather his feelings of discomfort. He was designed to be most comfortable with being the person that he is and he will never be happy until he accepts himself as he is. Even should he mistakenly think that he cannot be happy being the person he is, he is wrong. Because God made him this way and he was designed to be happy the way he is.

He needs to learn to trust that God means well for him, that if God died for him on the cross, then he knows that God's love is real and that whatever he needs to live in peace, God will eventually provide him with. And what God will provide will surpass the desires of human beings.

The gender that a person has in life, the person will have it forever. They will be the same people in heaven as they were on Earth, although in a glorified and sinless way; they will be restored to the original perfection that they were created with.

Additional things can be given to them, but they don't lose what they had originally. It doesn't matter whether we are speaking of the normal person, the homosexual, the person with Down syndrome – all are like this.

Whatever a person needs to be happy – in heaven, they will have. If it really is impossible for the person to be happy unless he is a member of the opposite sex, then such will be given to them. But, in reality, this doesn't exist, because God knows what makes him happier better than he does and the person he was designed to be happiest as, is his own self.

If a person has interests in things traditionally reserved for the opposite sex, there is nothing wrong with pursuing these things, so long as scandal is avoided. But he has to be himself. He can't try to be someone different, because he is uncomfortable with himself.

It is possible that a person can have genuine interest in things traditionally reserved for the opposite sex, or there are kinds of behaviour that are natural to the person, which are traditionally thought of as belonging to the opposite sex.

And there may be people who find it offensive for him to have these interests or have this kind of behaviour, but that doesn't mean it is wrong in itself. What is wrong is if he refuses to accept himself because he is not comfortable with himself. Rejection of self, is rejection of God.

Now, if his natural feelings and personality really are completely the same and identical as how a girl feels and how her personality is, then he must accept this nature as well and live accordingly... but I have great doubts that this is really the case with virtually anyone.

If you took a normal heterosexual girl and raised her as a boy, she thought of herself as a boy and followed male role models as a child, and you altered her brain with male hormones during her development adolescence, and she reached adulthood and wanted to be like other women, she would never have the same personality as a normal woman and if she tried to do so, she would need to reject herself in order to do so, because that is not what she is and what she developed to become.

By the same logic, even if what I theorize about the hidden gender is true and that there are some boys that have female souls and vice-versa, such people could perhaps never be the same as typical males and females. If you had a boy with a homosexual attraction from biology who in fact had a female soul, and you raised him as a boy, he got testosterone at puberty, he had male role models growing up and was treated as a boy; even if he ultimately is a girl, he will most likely never have the same personality as a normal female, either.

And there is nothing wrong with that.

He is living out a feminine vocation in his own way, which is just as equally feminine as any normal woman, although human thinking may think differently. He doesn't need to change himself to become like normal women in order to be feminine anymore than does a normal woman need to change herself to be more like him in order to be feminine. The femininity of each one is shared equally – assuming the hidden gender is real. And if he were to try to change himself to make himself more like what he thinks a true woman is, he would be rejecting himself and that would have to be condemned.

Keep in mind, as I've already stated, this is not just for this issue of transgenderism but is also for all people. Human beings throughout the history of the world have continually imposed gender roles on men and women which are actually opposed to who they are.

Women who were very interested in learning and yet

told that this was not feminine, and so they suppressed their true interest, rejected their true nature and thus rejected the Creator who made them. Men who were very emotional and were told that this was not masculine and so they suppressed this, rejected their true nature and thus rejected the Creator who made them. It is not for human beings to decide what is femininity or what is masculinity, but it is for them to look at the architecture and artwork made by the Creator and to accept it (and give glory to it and thanks for it) as it was given.

Whether it be in the 21st century, the 19th century or a thousand years before Christ, people in all times have done exactly what I warned about above by not being the people that they are in order to be a man or a woman according to the society's definition imposed upon them, and this is wrong, because it is a rejection of their true identities and a rejection of the Creator who made them.

The tendency to reject our own natures is another part of the consequences of original sin, which works itself throughout history and civilization. We think that there is something wrong with who we are, we reject the nature God gave us and fight against it, and God calls back to us 'Who told you that you were naked? Did you eat from the fruit of the tree that I told you not to eat?'

The bottom line is that people must be themselves, and

accept how God made them. This includes the body as well.

If a person wants to dress in clothing of the opposite sex or take on the appearance of the opposite sex, he can do so, as long as it is not masturbation and he is avoiding scandal, whether or not he is transgendered. However, under no circumstances can the person permanently alter his body for this purpose, because rejection of the body is rejection of the Creator.

He cannot mutilate himself or do anything to the body that will permanently change it. In the bible, Moses did not permit the Israelites to cut or tattoo themselves.

It is morally permissible to remove a part of the body if doing so is necessary for some important medical reason, wherein the health of the body is going to suffer unless this part is removed. Mutilation in that event is permissible, since you are not really mutilating the body but rather you are doing something to prevent further loss in bodily function (or restore something that was already lost).

People who get an appendix removed need to do so or else they might die, and hence the removal of the flesh is not mutilation but it is the prevention of further mutilation and damage from occurring. People who have gangrene in injured limbs can have the limbs removed because the gangrene can threaten to spread and cause further loss in bodily function, and so mutilation is acceptable in such a circumstance.

But without this need, mutilation is not acceptable, because you are removing something that God gave to you.

In science fiction, the idea is often explored of human beings surgically altering their bodies with machinery or replacing body parts with technology. And in science fiction, sometimes people have mechanical limbs or mechanical bodies that function even better than the bodies they were born with.

In the future, even if such a thing were possible and you could replace a body part with a machine that could do the same functions and even more, the church's teaching would still condemn this.

Even if you could replace your arm with a mechanical arm that had all the same feeling, could do all of the same things and was even stronger and more durable than your ordinary arm, this couldn't be accepted by the church unless a serious medical reason required it.

But why?

Because that is not the arm that God gave to you. The arm that God gave to you is perfect, but when you are removed from paradise, it doesn't seem perfect because it was designed for paradise and you are living in exile.

The arm that God gave to you is perfect, it is the one
that is designed for you- it is the one that you were
designed to be most satisfied with. But the machinery is
not perfect, it was not designed for you and it is not the
one you were designed to be most satisfied with.

It doesn't matter whether you think that being
stronger, being more durable or anything like this makes
an arm superior to another arm··· because you are just
a human being and you do not understand the mind of
God. What He gave to you was a perfect arm, designed
for you, and there is nothing else that you can replace it
with, which is superior to that.

So, even if science fiction could be made a reality, and
we could cut off your arm and put a robotic arm on you,
which did everything your arm could do, and it was
stronger than your arm, and could shoot laser beams
from its fingers or deflect bullets with powerful magnets
at the elbows, etc. -the church would have to condemn
this kind of surgery, because your original arm was
perfect and you are replacing it with something
imperfect made by human beings.

If you understand this, then you know what then has to
be said about the issue of transsexual surgery.

Even if people really are born as men in women's
bodies or women in men's bodies, the body they have

is still theirs and even if you could permanently change it with surgery, you are taking something perfect and replacing it with something made by human beings. Hence, even if transgenderism is true, this surgery is still not permissible.

What about the hormones? Technically, these hormones are only causing the body to grow in different ways, and they don't necessarily need to destroy anything in the body. They use natural processes within the body itself to cause this growth and alteration. However, the changes they make are still permanent.

I am not sure I can safely answer that question. I don't think it is necessarily mutilation, but that doesn't mean it is God's will.

Eating lots or little food will also alter the body's shape. Body-building will alter the body's shape. Sexual activity will permanently alter the brain. But this isn't mutilation; the body is just changing to a different shape through a natural process, rather than being altered artificially.

Mutilation implies an artificial alteration – one where human beings are destroying something made by God in order to make the shape according to human will. In this case, it is not mutilation, because it is the body's own process that is occurring and if the man starts to have breasts, those breasts are then part of his true body that

God gave to him. All that occurs in the body as a natural development should be understood as being the body that God gave to the person.

The hormones are an artificial addition, but the actual response to the hormones that causes the breasts to form is in fact a natural process that occurs in the body itself, which is why I write this way.

If the man later had surgery to remove those breasts, it would then actually be mutilation, since he was then cutting off something that God gave to him. Similarly, belly fat and wrinkles are also part of the person's true body that God gave to him. The person is then obligated to accept his breasts, to accept his wrinkles or accept his belly fat, just as he must accept the rest of the body that God gave to him.

If someone were to have surgery to remove the fat, it would also be mutilation. However, if a natural process was used to remove the fat, then it would not be a mutilation.

To accept it, means that one must accept it is part of oneself.

It doesn't have to mean that the person is not allowed to desire the state of his body without these things, however. The body can go through many changes in the lifetime of the person, and it is not wrong for a boy to have a desire for his present body to someday change and become a man's body. This is normal.

If the boy desires his body to change and become a different body, it is not wrong, but if he rejects his current body while doing so, then it is wrong. If he wants to be a man so badly that he rejects the current body of the child he has, then this is a sin.

A person with belly fat is permitted to desire to one day have a body without the belly fat, but he is not permitted to reject the body with the belly fat he has currently and think it is something shameful. He might feel ashamed of perhaps living an unhealthy lifestyle that led to him accumulating such fat, but he should not be ashamed of the body itself.

The body is good, no matter how many fat cells it may have. Every fat cell was created by God as an act of goodness. The commandment to take care of our own health may dictate that people who have large numbers of fat cells ought to try to exercise and diet more in order to have a healthier weight, but that doesn't mean that the body with the fat cells is in itself an evil thing that should be rejected. It is merely a good thing that ought to change into another good thing, because the commandment dictates that such a change ought to take place and not because the first body was evil.

If the person uses a natural process to eliminate the belly fat (eg. Dieting and working out), then it is not mutilation or rejection of self, but it is the use of a natural process to change one good body into another good body, which hopefully will be a healthier body than the previous one. It is not mutilation.

In my opinion, I think that the hormone therapy is also not mutilation for the same reason, since the changes it induces in the body are a natural process that makes the body naturally change from one shape to another.

If some natural process could be found that could alter everything else in the body, and cause the brain, the sex organs, to all change to that of the opposite sex, then it would also not be mutilation for the same reason. It would be a natural change of a good body into another good body. It would not have to imply a rejection of what God had created.

But even if it is not mutilation, there are other reasons to think about here in answering the question of whether or not such therapy is morally licit.

In answering this question, one would have to consider 'human ecology' and how it was that God planned for the human being to live.

Firstly, it has to be realized that transgendered people typically want to transition because they want to live the life of the opposite sex. This is not always true, but as a generality it is often true.

However, the reality is that they are reaching for something that cannot be attained with such a method.

The hormone therapy will change the shape of the body

and will affect the personality of the person going through it, but it does not change the person completely into the opposite sex. Most importantly the brain is not going to become the same brain as the opposite sex possesses.

Even if the things I said before about the hidden gender are true, I should note that I don't think that this means that such a person is able to take up the same gender roles as a person of the opposite sex.

If a man had a brain that was sexually designed for other men, and even if he had natural qualities in his personality that were seemingly feminine, that doesn't mean that he has the same brain as a biological woman. It is very likely that he doesn't. She has things in her brain that makes her more suited for feminine roles, and he may not have those things, even if he has a brain designed sexually for men. Even if he is actually a she, and he has a female soul, he can't really live his life as an ordinary woman, and be happy in it, because he was not designed for that.

For example, perhaps he was designed to be attracted to males, but he never possessed the instincts that make women good with babies or children. Or he might have feelings that are seemingly more feminine, but he doesn't actually feel emotionally comfortable with being in the role of a wife to a husband, since those instincts that normal women possess were never coded into his brain.

Hormone therapy is perhaps not enough to change this. If some kind of natural process could be found that could actually render the man's brain to completely change into a feminine one, then these problems are then theoretically solved.

The hormonal therapy therefore, while not being mutilation, may still be inadvisable for people, even if they really are the opposite sex in disguised, simply because the therapy is meant to help the person take on the appearance of the opposite sex in society, but the person is incapable and would actually be unhappy to try to fulfill that role, since he doesn't possess the same things that the opposite sex has in order to fulfill those things and be happy in it.

He can try hard to live his life as a woman and yet he will never actually have what he is seeking, because the design inside of him makes him designed for something different. He could be the opposite sex in disguised, he could truly have a female soul, and yet his vocation and design does not make him well-designed to live life in a typical female role, the same as normal women.

If he possesses the hidden gender, then he is just as equally feminine as they are- he possesses the gifts and vocation of femininity just as equally as any normal woman does — he doesn't need to become like them in order to be a true woman any more than they need to become like him in order to become true women. But he is different from them, and he can't live the same way as they do, nor can they live the same way that he does, and this is not really a problem either.

The same things are obviously all hypothetically true for females with male souls.

Hence, even if he didn't mutilate himself, and just used hormone therapy and wanted to take on the appearance of the opposite sex in order to completely live as a member of the opposite sex, this may not be well suited to his nature, since even if he has the hidden gender, he can never actually be the same as what is trying to imitate, since he possesses different talents.

Now suppose if the person does not want to try to live as a member of the opposite sex, but they want to live simply as themselves in their own unique way, neither as an ordinary biological woman would live, nor as a biological man would live; and they want to go through the hormone therapy, just because they think they would be happier with these changes happening in their bodies. In this case, it could be morally acceptable, but there are a few other considerations to take into account.

The therapy produces some permanent changes and it may have negative impacts on certain parts of the body. It is also suggested that it increases the risk of cancer – although a doctor could explain this better than I could.

If those negative impacts can be mitigated and the

person has made careful discernment about whether this is the right thing for them or not, then perhaps I am wrong, but I don't think there is any longer any objection in that case to the person going through the therapy or transitioning to the opposite sex, so long as everything written above continues to be borne in mind.

If a heterosexual man who did not think of himself as a woman wanted to take female hormones, not to be something that he couldn't, but for some other odd reason for why he wanted those changes to occur in his body, he wouldn't be necessarily barred by the commandments from doing so, as long as all the considerations I wrote about are being adequately answered. If that is true for him, then a hidden gender person who wanted to take such hormones, also wouldn't necessarily be barred either.

If the transitioning person is wearing clothing of the opposite sex in a manner that is neither sexual or scandalous, if no mutilation is involved in the process, if the person is seeking interests and acting with behaviours that are natural to his true self and not things he pursues because he can't accept his true self, if he is not harming his health or harming the lives of other people by what he does, then I think there is nothing wrong with transgender transitioning in that case. Even if the person doesn't have the hidden gender and wants to transition, there is nothing wrong it, theoretically, so long as those conditions are met.

Besides this, however, we can actually list many ways in the modern world where people reject their bodies and try to change it according to their desires.

There are many people who go through plastic surgery, breast enhancements, or some other kind of permanent artificial modification to the body in order to find the appearance that they are looking for. This has to be condemned for the same reasons that transsexual surgery is: because they are taking the perfect body God gave to them and exchanging it for something imperfect made by human beings.

Liposuction that is being done for cosmetic rather than urgent medical reasons also would have to be condemned for the same reason.

Even smaller things like piercings or tattoos would have to be condemned also because they are permanently changing the body in an artificial way. Moses told the Israelites that they could not cut themselves or give themselves tattoos.

Laser eye surgery, which has to destroy and alter tissue in order to improve sight, I think also would have to be condemned, since it is not actually restoring the health of the eye, it is just changing the shape of the eye by damaging it to give it better vision. The eye, as an organ and not as a tool of vision, is actually less healthy after the surgery than before. It sees better, but there are parts that are damaged that will function less well than before.

I suppose many might disagree with this opinion of mine, but I would ask: what is the difference between that and destroying the health of some other part of the body in order to achieve a better function that I desire to have? For example, if I can run faster by cutting off some flesh in my body, which I think I don't need, in order to make the body lighter, is it OK? How is this any different from achieving the function of beauty by mutilating some part through plastic surgery that I think is impairing that function?

Surgical procedures to prevent a person from having any more children, also have to be condemned for the same reason.

The only cosmetic changes that are morally permissible are those which do not require destroying something in the body. If you cut your hair, or file your nails, they will grow back; furthermore, the hair and the nails are not living anyways and they are just protrusions of dead organic material coming out of your body. It is OK to alter these things, because you are not losing something in the body that God gave to you.

If such a mutilation is necessary to do or else some serious medical consequence can result and there is no alternative, then it is permissible because by doing so you are guarding the rest of the body from damage. But if it is for cosmetic reasons only, all that would be morally permissible would be something that you can add on top of what is already there without destroying anything in the body.

Imagine if God Himself came down from heaven one day and gave you an ordinary stone, without saying anything else, and then went back to heaven again. And suppose the same day you visited a cosmetic surgery clinic, and one of the staff members gave you a diamond. In human eyes, just looking at the two objects, the diamond might be appraised at a higher value than the stone, but in reality, which of the two was the greater value?

If any of the pieces of furniture made by Jesus survived to today and they could be identified, and these pieces of furniture were just ordinary in appearance, would they be a lesser value than the fine furniture that gets sold at auctions for millions?

If you understand this, then you should be able to know what the objection to this surgery is.

If we were to go back to the science fiction for a moment⋯ if someone invented something that went over the skin or over the body, and gave a person all these abilities that the robotic limb had, but the body was still left intact, there would be nothing wrong with this. If something could be surgically attached to the body, but without altering the body and allowing the possibility for it to be detached, this would be permissible.

But you could never destroy what was already there in order to do this, because the body God gave to people was perfect.

All people, regardless of whether we are speaking of homosexuality or just all people in general··· all people, need to accept themselves for who they are and not to try to fight against it. They must accept their bodies, they must accept their personalities, and they must accept their desires; they shouldn't reject these things because either they or other people do not like these things. They must understand that everything that looks like it is something for evil, is actually something good in disguise, but because we live in exile, it is often hard to see.

Rejecting any of these things is a rejection of the Creator, it is a sin against 'human ecology'.

Now, after all that has been said, however, what do we say about the people who really do want to be members of the opposite sex and who perhaps even wish more than anything that they could be a member of the opposite sex? And this desire, no matter what, will just not go away? Whether speaking of people with a hidden gender or those without it, this phenomenon exists.

Everything I wrote above about the need to accept one's own self is true. The way that God made us is good, and we need to accept that, even if we crave for something else.

However, suppose that someone accepts themselves, they believe that the way that God made them is good, but they still wish they could become the opposite sex. They don't reject who they are, but they want to have something else that they didn't have before. What do we say in response to this desire?

All desires are created by God and are good. It is just that people do not see the thing that they actually desire, and instead think that what they appear to desire is what they want, when in fact the true answer to their desire is something more than what their hearts were set on.

If people desire to be the opposite sex, this desire is good, because all desires are good, but it is not necessarily the case that this desire is fulfilled by becoming the opposite sex. The desire may be designed for something more, but within the blindness that original sin places upon us, we fail to see the higher thing that our desires are really trying to find.

In Revelations it says that God will wipe away every tear in the end. There will be nothing in heaven that will not be fulfilled for people. Hence, we know that no matter what thing that people desire on Earth, in heaven they will get the satisfaction that they need. Hence, whatever this desire, as God created it, is truly answered by, the people who have this desire will get that satisfaction in heaven. Whether this is done by actually changing their sex as they wish or giving them something more than that, which they didn't realize was what they really wanted, the bottom line is that what they will have an answer to it if they are patient and hope in God.

Cross-dressing and hormones are not capable of making a person the same as if they were born as a member of the opposite sex. Whether or not some technology will be invented someday that would make it possible, I am not sure. But regardless of whether or not human efforts could do it, is it possible that God could change the sex of a person in heaven who wanted to be a member of the opposite sex?

Whatever you had on Earth that was good, you will not lose it in heaven. The body we have, the personality we have, we will have in heaven as well. But that doesn't mean that we cannot have things in addition to this as well. The body of the person born without eyes is good and he will have it in heaven, but doesn't mean God couldn't let him also enjoy a body with eyes in heaven in addition to the body without eyes.

With gender, however, there is a profound issue involved in this that has to be answered to understand this issue.

In the gospel when James and John go to Jesus to request that they be allowed to sit at his right and his left, He replies that this is not His to give but it is for those that the Father has prepared it.

The Father created every person with a vocation. We could also call it a 'name', a purpose or a calling. It means that each person was created by the Father to do something that fulfilled part of the Father's plan for the world. It was not the vocation of James and John to sit at Jesus' left and right, but it was for someone else. Jesus Himself does not have the power to change human vocation, because it is fixed by the Father.

Gender is intimately tied together with vocation and forms an intrinsic part to it. Male and females have different vocations from each other and they are not interchangeable.

Vocation is from God, and not even Jesus has the power to change it. Gender is also an intrinsic part of vocation. The vocation that was given to the Virgin Mary, that was given to the apostles, that was given to me or you or anyone else is something that came from the Father and which no power in heaven or earth has the ability to rewrite. The person can choose to follow the vocation they are given or not, but to change the calling and purpose that they had in this world that came from the Father is not within the power of any human being to do, including Christ Himself.

I wrote that if one could change the sexual preferences of the brain, then one could change the gender, however, that doesn't mean that change of gender is then possible. God rules over all Creation and if He determines that the brain cannot be changed in that way, then it will not be changed in that way.

If one could biologically cure aging and prevent any disease or injury from touching a person, then the person will have cheated death. But if God determined that the person should die, then it will mean that people will not be able to both cure aging and prevent disease or injury from coming.

Because vocation is something from the Father and is not alterable by any power, I have difficulty imagining how it could actually be possible to change the gender of the person, since if you did so, it would mean that you changed the vocation.

Is it possible that you could have a vocation that expressed itself through either gender?

Although I am not certain of this, I have difficulty believing it. I believe that male and female vocations are fundamentally different. One has a vocation to human beings and to do the work with human beings, and the other has a vocation to God and to do the work with the rest of creation. One is the image and glory of human beings, and the other is the image and glory of God. I think it is impossible to have a vocation that expresses itself through both. I invite the reader to read my book *Witchcraft* to understand more of what I think about it.

The 'name' of the person given by the Father, or in other words, the vocation of the person given by the Father, in the spiritual world, is like the speed of light in the laws of physics. Time and space can bend, but light is always constant. All other things can potentially change, but vocation is unalterable by any power.

That being said, I could imagine some ways that gender could seem to change without breaking vocation and that would open up the possibility of whether God could change the sex of a person in heaven.

If what I wrote about the hidden gender is true, then that means that it is possible for someone to possess the soul of the opposite sex in their spiritual dimension, which is manifested in their physical body by the part of the brain that deals with sexual preference, even if every other part of their body belongs to the sex they seem to have been assigned.

Hence, if that is true, it is then possible for a person to have the personality and body of the opposite sex, and they still retain their gender and vocation as a member of their own sex. A man with a female soul will have a brain designed sexually for men, even if he has a personality and body that largely contains most or all of the attributes that are normally associated with masculinity. A woman with a male soul will have a brain designed sexually for women, even if she has a personality and body that largely contains most or all of the attributes that are normally associated with femininity.

Vocation is not broken by this. The man with a female soul was never actually a male, but just had attributes that were associated with masculinity. He was always a female, he was always the image and glory of man rather than image and glory of God, he was always the weaker sex, the human being was always his head rather than God being his head, he always retained a female vocation designed for people and work with people rather than for God and work with all other parts of the creation. The masculine attributes he seemed to possess never negated this and his vocation was never violated.

The female with a male soul was never actually a female, but she just had attributes that were associated with femininity. She was always a male, she was always the image and glory of God rather than the image and glory of man, she was always the stronger sex, she always had God as her head rather than human beings as her head, she always had a male vocation to serve God through labour in the creation rather than a vocation designed for people. The feminine attributes she seemed to possess never negated this and her vocation was never violated.

If Leonardo da Vinci had a female soul, then his work in making all of his art can be interpreted as the way that he served as a companion to human beings. He creates such beautiful things to please human beings, like how Eve was created to be a companion to please Adam. The same is true of every other great male artist had hidden female souls – they were doing their work to be companions to human beings, as true daughters of Eve, by pleasing the senses of human beings by the beauty that they created and doing the work for the human being. Their head is human beings, their head is not God; it is human beings that they were given their talents to please. God doesn't care if the painting or the dance is beautiful or ugly – all is beautiful to Him.

Now, if all that about the hidden gender is true as I personally suspect, then it means that you can be a member of the opposite sex without breaking vocation, although you never actually are a member of the opposite sex. And therefore, if someone wanted to be the opposite sex in heaven, God could change a woman into a male with a female soul or change a man into a female with a male soul, just as the hidden gender person is, containing the body and personality of the opposite sex, but just without ever actually being the opposite sex, and vocation would not be broken by this.

Obviously, if it is the hidden gender person that desires to be a member of the opposite sex, so that the male with a female soul wants to be female, then vocation is not violated either by turning him into a woman and in his case, he would actually be a true woman with a female vocation and sexuality, just as he had before when he was a male with a hidden gender.

Now, if God did change such people in heaven, I don't think it would mean that the person would necessarily lose what they had before. The person born blind will have both the blind state and the state with eyes in heaven. The person who got to be the opposite sex in heaven would still retain what they had on Earth in addition to what they gained as new.

If God changed such people, then both what they had before and what they had later remain part of them, both are beautiful and good, and both are reflections of the same vocation given by the Father.

I obviously can't say if God does that in heaven or not. What I do know for certain is what I wrote before that all tears are wiped away and all things will have an answer. If the only way for the people to have their tears wiped away is by being the opposite sex, then they will be the opposite sex; if the person does not require this to have their tears wiped away because God prepared something even greater for the person, then that person will not be the opposite sex. Whatever the person needs to be fully satisfied, they will have in heaven – that is a reality, even if we cannot see how it should happen now.

God has prepared things for us that are far beyond what we hope for and imagine.

We know this because Paul said that what the eye has not seen, what the ear has not heard and what no heart has conceived is what the Father has prepared for those who love Him. Hence, the people in this life now that badly wish they could be the opposite sex – no matter what, you know that in heaven God will provide them whatever it is that they needed to be satisfied – whether it was what they thought they desired or what they didn't think they desired, God has the answer to what they need to be satisfied and they can put all of their trusts in this, and they will not be disappointed.

And even if God did give to them as they thought they desired, then they still have to accept that they are the people they are now and realize that this is a good thing.

In China, there is a popular contemporary song called 'Little Apple' (小苹果）sung by the Chopsticks brothers （筷子兄弟）. As I mentioned before with Britney Spears, all forms of art have their own interpretation in heaven.

The music video starts by showing a girl with her boyfriend sitting at a table and the girl asks the boy (in Korean) if she is pretty, and he retorts several times with annoyance 'is appearance important?' And she, unhappy, then goes to a plastic surgery clinic and when the bandages are removed she has a man's face (It's the face of one of the two chopsticks brothers).

The song then begins by showing the duo as Adam and Eve (with one of the men having his hair long like a woman) under the tree of the knowledge of good and evil. The snake appears with a red and white banded pattern telling them to eat, and they do eat. A group of female dancers then appears being led by a beautiful red-headed woman who is dressed in clothes that are the same pattern as the snake that led them into temptation.

The video then goes on to show the duo as being dressed like European colonists on a tropical island (with one as a man and the other as a woman), and then as a couple during the Korean war when the man goes to fight and doesn't come home because he is killed. The same lyrics are repeated throughout the video.

I think the tree of the knowledge of good and evil, perhaps was just an ordinary fruit tree, but God told the humans not to take any fruit from it. In the revelations of Bridget of Sweden, she said that it was an apple tree, which modern popular culture also seems to have assumed – perhaps at the Spirit's inspiration, because the Spirit will plant seeds in cultures.

There was nothing different from this apple tree versus any other apple tree, and if the humans wanted to eat apples they could get them from anywhere.

But the snake told them that by eating this fruit they could become like God. Eve desired it then. She had not yet eaten the fruit, however, and so she was not under the deception of concupiscence yet, which meant that her desire to be like God had not been corrupted and it was a good desire given to her by God. But God's plan was not for this desire to be fulfilled at this time and in this way.

The devil told her that God was hiding something from her and that the only way her desire could be fulfilled was by disobeying Him and eating this fruit. She didn't trust that God's plans for her were good, she didn't trust in God's love and so she ate it.

She gave it to her husband and he ate. They ate the apples, and they tasted just like ordinary apples because they were nothing more than just ordinary apples.

But, what they didn't understand is that they had now abandoned God's plan and decided to follow their own plan instead. The knowledge of good and evil was this: that human beings should follow their own plans and not God's plan, that they should decide for themselves what is good and what is evil, and not God deciding for them.

The Creation was perfect, the human being perfect, everything was perfect. But if you take something perfect and do not use it the way it was meant to be used, it will not seem like it is perfect.

Imagine a car. The engineers who designed and built the car build it in a certain way, and you need to follow their instructions in order for the car to work correctly. And if their instructions are followed, then the car will run fine. But imagine someday someone buys the car and they refuse to listen to the engineers and insist on their own method. They say, 'I am not going to let these engineers tell me how my car works; I will decide myself how it works!' And so rather than filling the car with gas, he decides to fill it with milk. Rather than using a key to open it, he tries to open it with a banana. Rather than using the accelerator to make the car move, he insists on taking a whip and scourging the car with it, to make it go forward. And once he tries all these things, and finds the car doesn't work, he then blames the engineer and he blames the design of the car, and says that the car is bad and that there is something inherently wrong with it.

Human beings are like this with the creation, including their own bodies. Everything God made was perfect and if all people follow His plans about how the Creation was supposed to be used, then no one would ever suffer anything.

When Adam and Eve took the apple, the apple was the same as any other apple, but once they had taken it, they were no longer following the plan of God. That was the knowledge of good and evil: it was to decide for yourself what is good and evil, rather than God. And all the suffering in the world and all the effects of original sin, exist because what was made perfect is not being used in the way that the Engineer designed it. Hence, every person in the world is born into a place that is not paradise, because their ancestors from Adam and Eve onward have all done things that didn't follow the plan of God, and when the children are born they are thus born into a place that isn't paradise and they seek evil, because they were designed for paradise and the evil is the only thing present that looks like paradise.

There is nothing wrong with them, there is nothing wrong with any part of them, but they are just not in the place they were supposed to be in, because their ancestors did not follow the plan of God.

When Adam and Eve hid themselves, it was because they experienced unwanted lust after they ate the fruit and thus departed from God's plan. Their lusts were not wrong, but they were not intended to be occurring in ways that they would feel discomfort and in ways against their own will. Why did they have these lusts after they ate the fruit?

Because they desired to become like God.

The human being was in fact designed to become like God, and in fact to become One flesh with God in the marriage in heaven. Athanasius said that God became man so that man could become God. The lusts they had on Earth were intended for marriage on Earth but they were the shadow, the copy of what is in heaven.

The time when their lusts found their true answer⋯ in the union of God in heaven, like Teresa's ecstasy⋯ that was the time when they were going to become like God, which is what Eve rightly desired. And so, they ate the fruit, and their flesh then desired something, which could only be fulfilled when they became like God.

They desired to become like God, but because it could not yet be given to them, they lusted. And human beings have lust written into their nature, not as a bad thing or as an animal trait, but as a reminder that they were made for more than just this.

And God comes and asks them, 'Who told you that you were naked? Have you eaten from the tree of which I told you not to eat?'

It was human beings who decided there was something

wrong about the way they were created; something shameful about their bodies and who they were. They departed from God's plan. God's plan was for everything to be perfect, but they departed from it and decided on their own that it wasn't perfect, starting with themselves. God didn't tell them that they were not perfect; they ate the fruit and decided good and evil on their own.

The people today who are rejecting themselves, whether rejecting their bodies or their identities, are deciding good and evil on their own. They are eating the fruit, rejecting God's creation of them as perfect and deciding for themselves what is good and what is bad.

In the Chinese music video, the symbol of this is here, whether it was intended or not.

The girl who goes to alter her body through surgery and the boy who wants to be a girl through surgery and hormones, are taunted by images like this beautiful dancing woman (dressed like the snake in the garden) to abandon God's plan for them and try to look like her.

There are so many young people getting plastic surgery done at clinics in South Korea, including not only the native population, but also huge numbers of people from the surroundings countries. It has the highest per capita rate of such operations done of any place in the world.

They can＇t accept the bodies and faces they have, so they need to get it changed. The snake offers the apple to the human being and tells him that if he takes it, he will get something that God isn＇t giving to him. The devil tells humans beings that God isn＇t going to give to them what they need to be happy, and that they must abandon His plan and follow their own in order to find what they are looking for.

And in just the same way, the boy who wants to be a girl or the girl who is not happy with her appearance is taunted by the image of the beautiful woman, and drawn to reject their bodies, almost like she is the snake telling them that only by rejecting nature and following their own design can they be happy.

After Eve takes the bite of the apple, she gives it to her husband and he bites and chokes, then almost like he is thinking back at a memory, the image of the tropical island appears with him and his wife as colonists on it. And she is trying to talk to him, but what she says sounds like gibberish to him and he keeps repeating （in English） 'what are you talking about?' and then she changes into a mermaid, and she disappears. He then tries to fish her from the ocean with an apple and he catches a different mermaid, more beautiful than his wife who sees him playing with this one from a distance.

The same woman as before then appears dancing, this

time in very sexual clothing.

In real life, why does the girl go to the plastic surgery clinic? Perhaps because her boyfriend is not satisfied with her. No matter what she says, it goes in one ear and out the other, as though everything she says is gibberish; it is her appearance that matters. And so, she has to make herself into a 'mermaid', because being a real person is not good enough. But he is not satisfied with this and they break up. He goes out to find her again but falls in love with a girl more beautiful than her, and she is heartbroken because being herself is not good enough for him. The woman dancing in the sexual clothing is like girls abusing their dignity and dressing immodestly, because they want to be loved.

What is it that made the woman eat this apple? The man thinks back on it, and recalls it was his lack of love for her.

She then stares at him with seeming infatuation and there is a voice praying to God asking to be more beautiful. Then you see two children playing in a street, who suddenly grow up and become adults, and the man goes off to war and gets killed.

The woman is heartbroken by this. But the person she really belongs to is not this man who can' t stay by her forever because he is mortal too, but the immortal One who created her and was always near her. What she had in Earth is just the copy, and what is in heaven is the original she was created for.

The lyrics of the song are almost like they are answering this whole problem, as though they were the words from the Creator to the beloved one He created, who is taking a bite out of this apple, because she didn't trust that God's love was real.

我种下一颗种子 (wo zhongxia yike zhongzi)

I planted a seed

终于长出了果实 (zhongyu zhangchule guoshi)

In the end, it grew into a fruit

今天是个伟大日子 (jintian shige weida rizi)

Today is a great day

摘下星星送给你 (zhaixia xingxing song'gei ni)

I pluck the stars and gift them to you

拽下月亮送给你 (zhuaixia yueliang song'gei ni)

I pull down the moon and gift it to you

让太阳每天为你升起 (rang taiyang meitian wei ni shengqi)

I make the Sun rise for you everyday

变成蜡烛燃烧自己只为照亮你 (biancheng lazhu ranshao ziji zhiwei zhaoliang ni)

I become a candle and light myself to shine on you

把我一切都献给你只要你欢喜 (ba wo yiqie dou xiangei ni zhiyao ni huanxi)

I take everything I have and offer it to you to make you happy

你让我每个明天都变得有意义 (ni rang wo meige mingtian dou biande you yi' yi)

You make my every tomorrow into something meaningful

生命虽短爱你永远 (shengming suiduan ai ni yongyuan)

Although life is short, I love you forever

不离不弃 (bu li bu qi)

Never ever abandon you

你是我的小呀小苹果儿 (ni shi wode xiaoya xiao pingguor)

You are my little little apple

怎么爱你都不嫌多 (zenme ai ni dou bu xianduo)

How to love you has no limits

红红的小脸儿温暖我的心窝 (honghong de xiaolian’r wennuan wode xinwo)

Your little red face warms my heart

点亮我生命的火 (dianliang wo shengming de huo)

Lighting the fire of my life

火火火火火 (huo huo huo huo huo)

Fire, fire, fire…

你是我的小呀小苹果儿(ni shi wode xiaoya xiao pingguor)

You are my little little apple

就像天边最美的云朵(jiu xiang tianbian zui mei de yunduo)

You are just like the most beautiful clouds in the sky

从不觉得你讨厌 (cong bu juede ni taoyan)

I never felt like I couldn’t stand you

你的一切都喜欢 (nide yiqie dou xihuan)

I love every part of you

有你的每天都新鲜 (you nide meitian dou xinxian)

Because of you my every day is fresh

有你阳光更灿烂 (you ni yangguang geng canlan)

Because of you the Sun is bright

有你黑夜不黑暗 (you ni heiye bu hei' an)

Because of you the darkness is not dark

你是白云我是蓝天 (ni shi baiyun wo shi lantian)

You are the white cloud and I am the blue sky

春天和你漫步在盛开的花丛间 (chuntian he ni

manbu zai shengkai de hua congjian)

In the spring I will walk with you in the flowers

夏天夜晚陪你一起看星星眨眼 (xiatian yewan

pei ni yiqi kan xingxing zhayan)

In the summer I will be with you at night to look

at the twinkling stars

秋天黄昏与你徜徉在金色麦田 (dongtian

huanghun yu ni changyang zai jinse maitian)

In the fall I will roam with you in the golden

wheat fields

冬天雪花飞舞有你 (dongtian xuehua feiwu you

ni)

In the winter, the dance of the snowflakes

because of you will be...

更加温暖 (geng jia wennuan)

...even more lively

你是我的小呀小苹果儿(ni shi wode xiaoya xiao

pingguor)

You are my little little apple

怎么爱你都不嫌多(zenme ai ni dou bu

xianduo)

How to love you has no limits

红红的小脸儿温暖我的心窝(honghong de

xiaolian' r wennuan wode xinwo)

Red little face brightens my heart

点亮我生命的火(dianliang wo shengming de

huo)

Lighting the fire of my life

火火火火火(huo huo huo huo huo)

Fire, fire, fire...

你是我的小呀小苹果儿 (ni shi wode xiaoya xiao pingguor)

You are my little little apple

就像天边最美的云朵 (jiu xiang tianbian zuimei de yunduo)

Like the most beautiful clouds of the sky

春天又来到了(chuntian you laidaole)

The spring comes⋯

从不觉得你讨厌 (cong bu juede ni taoyan)

I never felt like I couldn't stand you

你的一切都喜欢 (nide yiqie dou xihuan)

I like every part of you

有你的每天都新鲜 (you nide meitian dou xinxian)

Because of you my every day is fresh

有你阳光更灿烂 (you ni yangguang geng canlan)

Because of you the Sunlight is even brighter

有你黑夜不黑暗 (you ni heiye bu hei' an)

Because of you the darkness is not dark

你是白云我是蓝天 (ni shi baiyun wo shi lantian)

You are the white cloud and I am the blue sky

春天和你漫步在盛开的花丛间 (chuntian he ni manbu zai shengkai de hua congjian)

In the spring I will walk with you in the flowers

夏天夜晚陪你一起看星星眨眼 (xiatian yewan pei ni yiqi kan xingxing zhayan)

In the summer I will be with you at night to look at the twinkling stars

秋天黄昏与你徜徉在金色麦田 (dongtian huanghun yu ni changyang zai jinse maitian)

In the fall I will roam with you in the golden wheat fields

冬天雪花飞舞有你 (dongtian xuehua feiwu you ni)

In the winter the dance of the snowflakes because of you will be...

更加温暖 (geng jia wennuan)

...even more lively

你是我的小呀小苹果儿(ni shi wode xiaoya xiao pingguor)

You are my little little apple

怎么爱你都不嫌多(zenme ai ni dou bu xianduo)

How to love you has no limits

红红的小脸儿温暖我的心窝(honghong de xiaolian'r wennuan wode xinwo)

Red little face brightens my heart

点亮我生命的火(dianliang wo shengming de huo)

Lighting the fire of my life

火火火火火(huo huo huo huo huo)

Fire, fire, fire...

你是我的小呀小苹果儿(ni shi wode xiaoya xiao pingguor)

You are my little little apple

就像天边最美的云朵 (jiu xiang tianbian zuimei de yunduo)

Like the most beautiful clouds of the sky

春天又来到了花开满山坡 (chuntian you laidao le huakai man shanpo)

The spring comes and the flowers cover the hillside

种下希望就会收获 (zhongxia xiwang jiu hui shouhuo)

Plant a seed of hope, and will reap a harvest

种下希望就会收获 (zhongxia xiwang jiu hui
shouhuo)

Plant a seed of hope, and will reap a harvest

你是我的小呀小苹果儿 (ni shi wode xiaoya xiao
pingguor)

You are my little little apple

怎么爱你都不嫌多 (zenme ai ni dou bu
xianduo)

How to love you has no limits

红红的小脸儿温暖我的心窝 (honghong de
xiaolian’r wennuan wode xinwo)

Your little red face warms my heart

点亮我生命的火 (dianliang wo shengming de huo)

Lighting the fire of my life

火火火火火 (huo huo huo huo huo)

Fire, fire, fire...

你是我的小呀小苹果儿(ni shi wode xiaoya xiao pingguor)

You are my little little apple

就像天边最美的云朵(jiu xiang tianbian zui mei de yunduo)

You are just like the most beautiful clouds in the sky

春天又来到了花开满山坡 (chuntian you laidao

le huakai man shanpo)

The spring comes and the flowers cover the hillside

种下希望就会收获 (zhongxia xiwang jiu hui shouhuo)

Plant a seed of hope, and will reap a harvest

The final and definitive truth about the questions I present in this book, I am not really sure. I could be wrong about the things I have theorized and speculated about here.

All I know for sure is that what this song says is the truth. All art has an interpretation in heaven, and this is the interpretation I give to it:

The human being wants to take a bite out of this little apple, because he doesn't trust God. He feels like God's plan isn't good enough and that God's way is not the way to be happy.

He creates so many perversions and abuses of his gift of sexuality, angering and crucifying the God who made

Him. Seeking his own way, instead of God's plan; taking the apple because he was deceived and thought God was hiding something from him.

The human being bites this apple, because he doesn't understand how much love God has for him. If the human being could see, even just slightly, just how much every part of his life matters so much to God, he would never dream of thinking that God and His law couldn't be trusted.

He bites the apple because he doesn't trust God's love for him, but in fact he was always the apple of God's eye.

Lord, we pray that you help us to accept ourselves as you created us to be. We pray that you help all of us human beings to realize that no matter what it feels like or what the world thinks, that you love us for who we are and you do not need us to become someone else. We pray that you help us to become what we were created to be and to reflect the divine light in whose image we are made in. We pray that through the merits of your Son's passion, we can be restored to what we have lost through sin. We ask for these things, if it is your will, in Jesus' name, Amen

All Glory to God